# ALL ABOUT ASHLAND

# ALL ABOUT ASHLAND

A Guide to the Oregon Shakespearean Festival

and Southern Oregon

*by Jane Lundin*

Ten Speed Press
Berkeley, California

1🜨
TEN SPEED PRESS
P.O. Box 7123
Berkeley, California 94707

Library of Congress Catalog Card Number: 88-50776
ISBN: 0-89815-282-8

Cover Design by Naomi Schiff
Book Design by Steve Herold
Typesetting by Lasergraphics

Printed in the United States of America

1    2    3    4    5    —    92    91    90    89    88

# Table of Contents

# About This Guide

A quarter of a million visitors every year can't be wrong. Ashland, Oregon is more than just a pretty little town in the middle of nowhere.

Crater Lake National Park, the Rogue River, the Jacksonville Historic District, the Oregon Shakespearean Festival and shopping were the top choices in a recent survey of area visitors reported in the *Ashland Daily Tidings* on October 23, 1987. Travelers from 48 states and 13 foreign countries took part in the survey and more than half gave Southern Oregon as their final destination.

Ashland is the home of a huge and renowned theatre festival — it's far more than just Shakespeare now — and a wealth of tourist facilities have been developed here as the festival has grown. There are two hotels, about fifteen motels and close to thirty bed and breakfast inns to stay in and almost seventy places to eat, from sidewalk stands to elegant French restaurants. Add to these the numerous restaurants and inns in nearby areas and the variety of interesting galleries and shops that have located in Ashland to serve visitors and it is clear that Ashland makes a delightful vacation headquarters.

The Visitors Bureau survey didn't include all of Southern Oregon's possibilities. Oregon Caves National Monument is also an easy day's trip from Ashland. For fishing and boating and white water adventures there are other rivers besides the Rogue, and numerous lakes as well. In addition to Historic Jacksonville, there are 75 properties in Jackson County that are listed in the National Register of Historic Places, 30 of them in Ashland itself. Besides the Shakespeare Festival, Ashland supports about ten other theatres and nearby Jacksonville is home to a family of summer music festivals. Southern Oregon State College, in Ashland,

1

is the site of the largest Elderhostel program in the country, providing stimulating academic experience and inexpensive vacations for hundreds of older people each year. If the survey had been done in winter, the skiing on Mt. Ashland would have been mentioned by many of the people who were interviewed.

There is another factor that brings visitors but wasn't part of the survey. By the standards of California's major cities and vacation areas, Ashland is a bargain. You will discover in the sections of this guide on lodgings and meals that the cost of living and vacationing in Oregon is modest. Most of the motel rooms are $50 or less, many a lot less, and winter rates are lower still. Most of the bed and breakfast inns charge between $45 and $65. There are inexpensive houses for big groups and families to rent, and the youth hostel charges $6 a night and has a kitchen.

But even if you don't cook, eating out is remarkably inexpensive. Good dinners can be had in Ashland for less than $10, even with a glass of wine included, and it's hard to spend $30. Theatre and music tickets are reasonable too. The current top price at the Shakespeare Festival is $18, and you will find all sorts of bargains described — previews, rush tickets, special matinees, standing room — that cut admission to as little as $5. Britt Music Festival tickets are similarly priced, and most of the other theatres charge less than $10. There's even Tightwad Tuesday, an Ashland merchants' promotion that makes bargain meals and movie tickets and other special savings available every week.

These are 1988 rates, but several factors work to keep prices from increasing. So many motels have been built that there are always empty rooms except on summer weekends; there is active price competition among them. The restaurants, unlike lodgings, depend on local patronage and must keep their prices in line with the local economy. The Shakespeare Festival also keys its prices to local patrons, and to the visiting family who will buy tickets to as many as nine plays for their week's vacation. Only in the bed and breakfast places does demand exceed supply. Increasing numbers of these inns are raising their rates to conform to what tourists pay in other areas.

I discovered Ashland in 1952 because my husband and I decided that the Shakespeare Festival would make a good wedding trip. I remember the town as quiet and timeless, set on the hillside between gentle fields and forested mountains, its residents going their way unruffled by a few summer visitors. Southern Oregon College made no impression on me at all; it must have seemed tiny compared to the University of California at Berkeley where we were both students, and it was on the edge of town then. I remember thinking that Lithia Park, on the other hand, was disproportionately grand and dramatic for such a sleepy place.

There was no freeway then and the forest seemed endless. We explored logging roads and nearby parks, visited Jacksonville, and saw four plays and a concert inside the walls of the old Chautauqua building, where once the circuit-riding lecturers brought culture to isolated townsfolk. We sat on park benches on the weedy, sloping ground, with only the sky overhead. We stayed in a cabin in Lithia Park that was one good shove away from collapsing, barbecued and picnicked to keep costs down, and ate a memorable meal at Omar's: steak and fresh peach pie. I even had my first legal drink in Ashland courtesy of a peculiar Oregon law, since changed, that let underage wives drink with their older husbands.

The festival was nothing grand, then. The stage was patterned after an Elizabethan theatre but was crudely built, and the costumes weren't the glamorous masterpieces they are today. The actors ranged from William Ball, who went on to lead the Actor's Workshop and ACT in San Francisco, and festival founder Angus Bowmer, to community people and amateurs. But the plays were exciting, performed without intermissions and at a faster pace than I had seen before.

All that was forever ago and nothing is the same anywhere, least of all in Ashland. When we returned, middle-aged and with half-grown children, we were overwhelmed by the growth of the festival. It was as if we had just looked in the mirror for the first time in twenty-five years. Since then we have returned every year and have seen more and more changes, in both the town and the Festival. As one lifetime resident said to me, "Sometime in the last ten years or so, Ashland went from being a community that enjoyed its summer visitors to being a tourist town," adding ruefully that no one who made a living in a shop on Main Street or a restaurant shared her qualms about the changes this had entailed. Certainly, the signs of increased prosperity are everywhere.

It is to help visitors cope with Ashland's ever-growing variety of places to stay and eat and things to do that this book is intended. We realized, my family and I, that we sometimes felt overwhelmed, even though we had been coming to the Festival for years. This guide is designed to help

3

visitors make the most of their stay in Ashland and broaden their experience of Southern Oregon. I hope you will discover Shakespeare and the Britt Music Festivals if you've come to fish, and get outdoors if you've come for the plays or the music. And I hope the information on lodging and restaurants leads you to places you enjoy.

There are lots of interesting guidebooks on the market that trace the author's choice of routes through some scenic area and describe the author's favorite places to stay, eat, shop and visit along the way, a few in each town. They make good reading, but to find them useful when traveling, you have to share the author's taste. When I read such books, I always wonder about the places that have been left out; were they actually inferior or just missed in the rush to get on to the next stop?

This isn't that kind of book. I have focused on Ashland, and have tried to include all the available lodging and eating places and attractions, with enough information for you to make choices that will meet your needs, not mine. As a long time consumer activist — I once was president of the largest consumer cooperative in this country — I truly believe that people have a right to facts on which to base their decisions. If it's worth fighting to get the ingredients listed completely on a dollar box of breakfast cereal, surely travelers deserve to know as much as possible before committing many dollars and their vacation time.

So this guide is not a directory, listing everything without evaluation, nor is it a list of my personal favorites, though I do have some after years of happy vacations in Ashland. The evaluations weren't made on a point system or by a committee, either. My tastes and interests are inevitably reflected in everything I've said, but I've tried to give you facts, along with my opinions. There are a few places in Ashland I can't recommend, and I've said why; there are many more that I found enjoyable, and I've detailed what pleased me about them.

All the restaurant and accommodation listings, with the exception of the out-of-town bed and breakfast places, are based on my visits in the fall of 1987. I stayed at many of the inns and ate at all the restaurants, and I did so without telling any of my hosts why I was there. I paid for all my meals and lodging; no free services were asked for or offered and no establishment has paid to be listed in this book.

In addition to meals and lodgings, I also investigated the recreational possibilities of this part of Southern Oregon. There is detailed information about both the Shakespeare and Britt Music Festivals which I hope will demystify the ticket ordering process a little, and help you take part in some of the other festival activities as well. Also included is information on the little theatres in and near Ashland and on other sources of music.

There are suggestions for day trips to the National Parks and Wildlife Refuges and to nearby lakes and recreation areas. Details of facilities for sports and outdoor activities, with telephone numbers to call for more information, are included. If pioneer history intrigues you, you will find museums and guided walks described and the National Register of Historic Places list for Ashland, grouped for easy touring. There is information on Elderhostel and other educational programs provided by the festivals and the college. There is also a section on shopping for fun, arranged as a series of walks.

Besides all this, I have included listings of services that might be needed by a traveler, from automobile dealers, banks and churches on through to veterinarians. I have not evaluated any of these; they are provided for your convenience. There is also a list of emergency numbers. I hope you make good use of every other part of the book, and enjoy Southern Oregon to the fullest.

---

### Telephone Numbers

**Calling from outside Oregon:**

The area code for the entire state of Oregon is **503**. That is the area code for all the telephone numbers in this guide unless another code is given with the number.

**Once you're in Oregon:**

You reach numbers outside your immediate area by dialing **1** before the number; if a recorded message interrupts to ask you to use the **1** you know you're making a toll call.

For directory assistance for any place in Oregon, you dial **1-555-1212**. Pacific Northwest Bell charges for each such call, even from pay phones.

### And Addresses

Ashland's zip code is **97520**. All addresses listed are in Ashland unless another city and its zip code are given.

The plaza in 1888, looking south. The mill was torn down to beautify the entrance to Lithia Park; the two closest brick buildings, the Bank of Ashland and the Masonic Hall, remain today. *Southern Oregon Historical Society*

The plaza more recently; since this picture was taken the plain looking, two-storey building in the center has been restored to look more as it did in the picture on page194 *Ashland Chamber of Commerce*

# *About Ashland*

## A Little History

Ashland was founded in 1852, recently enough that traces of the pioneer families are still easy to find. There are street names, and memorial plaques in Lithia Park, and if you take one of the walks sponsored by the Historical Society you'll see their houses, some of them still occupied by their descendants.

A succession of influences shaped the town. Gold, discovered in Jacksonville, brought the first people while fertile land and commercial opportunities attracted more permanent settlers. The railroad, culminating in the completion of the route over the mountains just one hundred years ago, brought in luxuries and contact with the outside and gave many people jobs. Chautauqua, the summer program of lectures and entertainment named for the first such program in Chautauqua, New York, drew people from surrounding districts to camp by Ashland Creek, starting a tradition of summer visitors. And Lithia water was a dream of prosperity as the Saratoga of the West that never materialized but gave the town its grand park.

The rerouting of the rail line in 1926 took many jobs away, and was followed by the national depression of the thirties. Radio and the movies made the Chautauqua obsolete. Soon the dome of the building that had housed it was pulled down as unsafe, leaving only the concrete walls. After World War II the Shakespeare Festival's expansion began to affect the town, bringing in more and more visitors with money to spend. In the sixties, the back to nature movement and its adherents brought ideas, particularly a commitment to handcrafts, that are still being felt. At the same time, Federal redevelopment policies almost cost Ashland its historic railroad district. Today, sentiment for preservation is combining

Ashland's grand depot, circa 1910; a picture of the dining room appears on page 173. *Ashland Public Library, print by Terry Skibby*

with the growth of the Festival to support the creation of bed and breakfast inns in old houses that would once have been torn down and the creative recycling of other structures as well.

Two of Ashland's major assets date from pioneer days. Southern Oregon State College has its roots in the Ashland College and Normal School which was opened in 1869 by a Methodist minister. In 1882, according to local historian Marjorie O'Harra, it became an official state normal school, with four teachers and 42 students in its two-year teacher training course. But state recognition didn't bring state money and the school closed its doors intermittently in its first twenty years and permanently in 1910. It was only reopened in its present location in 1926, but with state support ever since, it has flourished.

Today Southern Oregon State College offers degrees in 42 fields of study to some 4300 regularly enrolled students on a modern campus and provides community educational and cultural programs to a similar number of people, including over a thousand Elderhostel participants each year.

Lithia Park started with the Chautauqua Association's eight acres. Ashland's leaders were determined to secure the benefits of Chautauqua, both educational and commercial. A bond issue was passed to purchase the land and the first building was constructed in 1893.

The women of Ashland were the driving force that made the park possible, first the Ladies Chautauqua Club, and then the Women's Civic Improvement Club. They raised money to beautify the Chautauqua grounds, campaigned successfully for the establishment of a city-owned park, and cleaned up the plaza themselves, with their own rakes and wheelbarrows, while the town debated how it should be done.

John McLaren, famous for developing Golden Gate Park in San Francisco, was hired in 1914 to landscape a new section of the park as part of the attempt to develop a mineral springs resort based on Lithia water. The resort never got started — the details as recounted in Marjorie O'Harra's history of the park, available from the park office for $1, make entertaining reading — but trees he planted are still growing.

The park commission, with the aid of generous gifts and bequests, has continued to enlarge and develop the park. An auto camp with tourist cabins was built and eventually removed. The deer park and zoo are also gone now, but two lakes with ducks and swans to feed remain popular attractions. A children's playground has been constructed and a wading area in Ashland Creek. There is a Japanese garden and one displaying roses, a band shell and a new path system, and much new landscaping has been done, particularly since the 1974 flood. Most recently, McLaren's grand lighted staircase and its fountain from the Panama Pacific Exposition have been restored.

The railroad, once so prominent in Ashland life, is all but gone. When you walk through the old railroad district you can feel the depression that started when the main line was rerouted. There are few new buildings and lots of vacant land, still. All that remains of the huge depot that once boasted a three storey hotel and a restaurant for two hundred diners is a one floor wing that is used as the freight station. Passenger service was discontinued in 1955; the few freight trains that still come through are a pale reminder of Ashland's history as a railway center.

Today Ashland is a college town and a retirement center as well as a tourist mecca, a community of families, businesses, schools and churches. About fifteen thousand people now enjoy the beautiful countryside and gentle climate that attracted the first settlers. If you want to find out more about the history that led to what you see today, Marjorie O'Harra has written two books in addition to the pamphlet on Lithia Park. They are *Ashland, the First 130 Years* and *Southern Oregon, Short Trips Into History*; both are available at Bloomsbury Books and the Tudor Guild Shop.

The Southern Oregon Historical Society has changing exhibits and a collection of photographs at the Chappell-Swedenburg House, located at 990 Siskiyou Blvd., at the corner of Mountain Ave. They also conduct guided walking tours of historic areas.

Two other sources of local historical lore are the Festival Exhibit Center and the Ashland Public Library. Short movies on the history of the Festival are shown at the Exhibit Center, and there are displays of old photographs. The Library, a bit of history itself, is a 1910 Carnegie gift. It also houses a collection of photographs as well as books and newspapers.

## GETTING HERE — AND GETTING AROUND

**Driving** — Most people come to Ashland by car, on the interstate freeway, I-5, driving south from Portland, Seattle and Vancouver or north from Los Angeles and San Francisco. From the coast, U.S. route 199 from Crescent City to Grant's Pass is the most direct road, while Oregon routes 66 and 140 reach Ashland from Klamath Falls and the east.

I-5 bypasses Ashland in a gentle curve that

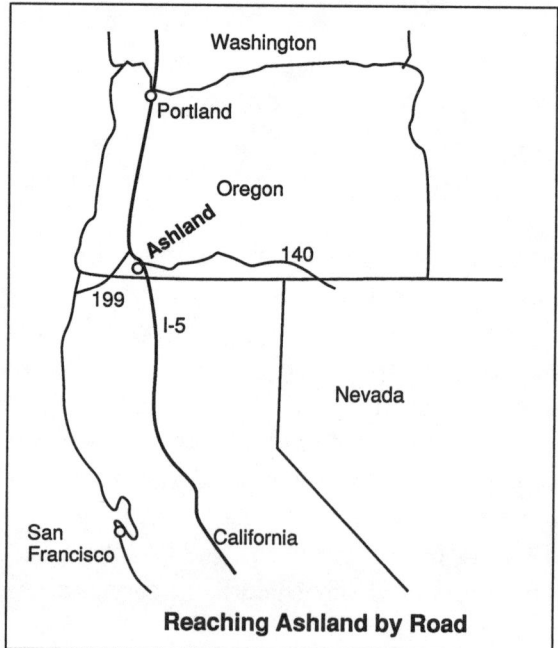

**Reaching Ashland by Road**

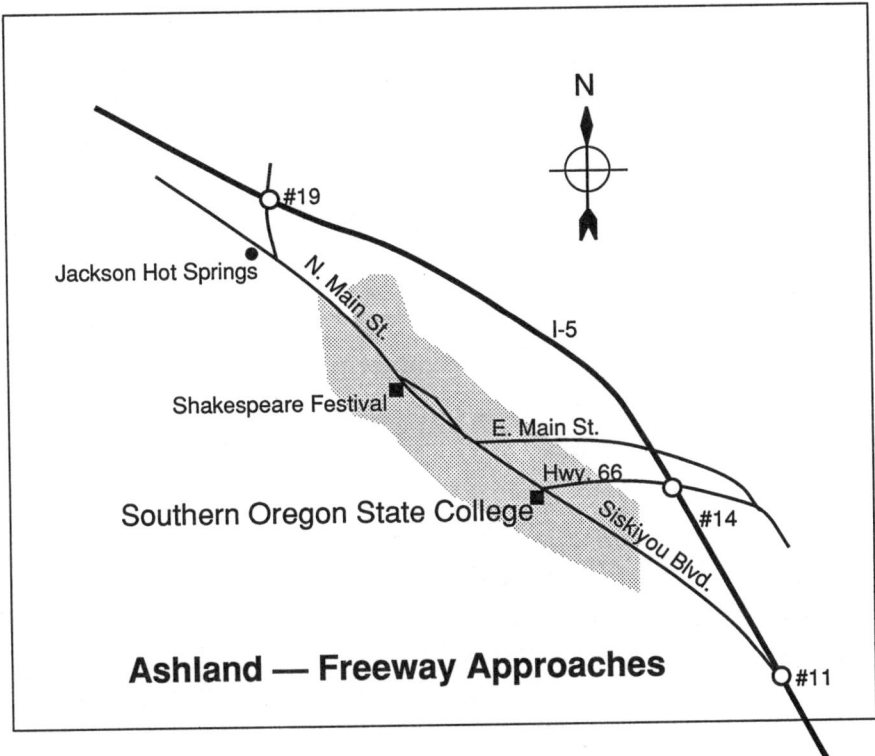

N

#19

Jackson Hot Springs

N. Main St.

I-5

Shakespeare Festival

E. Main St.

Hwy. 66

Southern Oregon State College

Siskiyou Blvd.

#14

**Ashland — Freeway Approaches**

#11

parallels the hills and the town stretched out along them. Three exits serve Ashland, numbered in terms of mileage from the California border, not consecutively. Heading north they are:

**#11** — The South Ashland interchange is accessible only if you're driving north and it lands you well south of town, on Siskiyou Boulevard. There is no development at this exit and no services are available, but there are a few motels far out on Siskiyou for which it is a convenient exit. Warning: this is not a complete interchange. You can enter the freeway going south only, and if you drive far enough out Siskiyou, you will find yourself doing so with no choice; it's 15 miles out of your way to turn around at the Mt. Ashland exit and come back.

**#14** — The Highway 66 interchange is where all the big new motels and gas stations have been built. Route 66, Ashland St., is developed all the way from the freeway to where it intersects Siskiyou Blvd., in the middle of the Southern Oregon State College campus. For anyone coming from the south, this is the most convenient exit for almost all of Ashland except the North Main area.

**#19** — The Valley View interchange is just north of the town line. You exit here onto South Valley View Road which crosses Highway 99, the continuation of North Main St., at Jackson Hot Springs. There are gas stations at this exit, along with a motel and the Department of Motor Vehicles Office. If your destination is north of the plaza, or if you're coming from the north, this is probably the most convenient route into town.

**Taking the train** — Though Ashland was a major railroad center for thirty years, there has been no passenger service since 1955. The nearest Amtrak trains stop at Klamath Falls, arriving from the south at 6:30 AM and from the north at 10:30 PM and leaving a 70 mile ride to arrange. It requires great dedication to rail travel to see this as a reasonable alternative. But for those who insist:

*Amtrak Reservations and Information*       800-872-7245

**Coming on a Bus** — Ashland is served by both Greyhound and Trailways buses. It's the slowest way to go, but the price is low. Service is available on routes going south from Vancouver and from Spokane, north from the major California cities, and west from Reno, with stops at intermediate towns. The bus station is at 91 Oak St., just off East Main and right in the heart of the downtown. Lots of accommodations, including the hostel, are within moderate walking distance, and Ashland Taxi operates out of the same office.

*Greyhound Bus Lines*       482-2516
*Trailways Bus System*       482-9250

**Flying In** — Commercial flights on United, Continental, P.S.A., and Horizon land at Jackson County Airport in Medford. From there it is approximately 15 miles to Ashland. Both bus and taxi service is available, and some of the motels in Ashland provide limousine service. There are also four car rental agencies in the airport. This is by far the most expensive method, but it certainly is easy and the airlines do offer round trip, advance-purchase fares that reduce the price considerably if you can match your plans to their restrictions.

*United Airlines*       800-241-6522
*Continental Airlines*       800-525-0280
*Pacific Southwest Airlines*       800-854-2902
*Horizon Air*       800-547-9308

If you fly your own plane, Ashland's Municipal Airport, Sumner Parker Field, has facilities described by the Chamber of Commerce as "3600 ft. paved and lighted runway with 70 tiedowns and a traffic pattern of 2700 feet. 80 and 100 octane fuel, mechanics and ground transportation available." The field is located just beyond the I-5 / Hwy. 66 interchange, on Dead Indian Road.

**Getting Around Without a Car** — Ashland Taxi has both individual cars and a shuttle bus that takes guests between their motels and the theatres. The shuttle costs $1 each way and can be booked by the motel office. The merchants have experimented with operating a motorized cable car to shuttle visitors between the motels and the downtown shops, but it is not clear whether it was considered successful enough to continue. Guests at the Ashland Hills Inn and the Flagship Quality Inn have access to free shuttle buses operated by the motels.

*Ashland Taxi*                                        482-3065

Rogue Valley Transportation District operates buses in and between the cities in Jackson County. A very detailed schedule with route maps can be picked up at the College's information office, the Chamber of Commerce, or from RVTD. No buses run on Sundays or major holidays. For information, contact:

*RVTD*                                          779-BUSS
*3200 Crater Lake Ave., Medford, 97504*

Bicycles can be rented from several places in Ashland; the details are listed in the section on Services (see page 224 ). Bike lanes have been established on some streets and, except for some steep hills in the residential area, the terrain is comfortably level.

**Renting a Car** — If you are planning to rent a car at the Medford airport, the following comparison of rates and terms, based on quotations given on 8/31/87 may be helpful. Even if rates have changed, it demonstrates the real savings to be had by shopping. The weekly rate for a small car was given as:

| | |
|---|---|
| *National* | *$128.95 prepaid, 25% cancellation penalty* |
| *Avis* | *$140* |
| *Sears/Budget* | *$205 (two weeks for $350)* |
| *Hertz* | *$219.97* |

All cars came with 700 free miles per week and cost between twenty and thirty cents a mile over that. All the companies offered 10% discounts to AARP members, business travelers, and frequent flyers, except on the special prices then available from National and Avis or on Budget's two week price. The Hertz agent told me with a perfectly straight face that her's was the lowest rate available; with all four offices lined up next to each other it is easy to see for yourself.

When you leave the airport for Ashland, go toward Medford, making a left at the stop sign onto Biddle Road. When you enter the freeway be prepared to move very quickly to the left for a left exit at the end of the overpass. Coming back from Ashland, the airport is at the second Medford exit. When you turn off the freeway prepare for an immediate left turn. From there it's all clearly signed.

If you take a taxi from the airport, you may be able to rent a car more cheaply from Butler Ford. As well as new cars, they rent used vehicles (for use within the Rogue Valley only) and motor homes. The cost for a used car is approximately $12 a day and 8 cents a mile with every eighth day free. Reserve well in advance; they don't have a big fleet.

*Butler Ford*                                                           *482-2521*
*1977 Highway 99 N*

**Not Getting Lost** — The problem with finding any place once you're in Ashland is that the street pattern looks like the grid we're all used to but really is full of irregularities. There are probably good reasons for each anomaly dating back to when the different sections of town were laid out, but together they add up to a lot of confusion for such a small place.

North of Helman St., North Main St. is rational enough. It goes roughly north out of Ashland and most of the side streets are numbered starting where they intersect it. Of course, it's the exceptions like West Hersey that cause confusion; it's numbered as if it ran (more or less) west from Helman. This is the oldest part of town and none of the streets line up exactly with the compass.

East of Fourth St., East Main goes roughly east, but Siskiyou Blvd. carries most of the traffic. Siskiyou cuts through the grid on the diagonal, creating triangular parcels. Most of the cross streets in this part of town run north and south; it's hard to go directly east or west without running into the high school or the college, so it's easy to get lost.

It's in the downtown area, between Helman and Fourth, that it gets really weird. At the plaza North Main turns a few more degrees toward the east and becomes East Main, when logically you would expect the other half of North Main to be South Main. Those streets which cross East Main are numbered out from both sides so that you have addresses

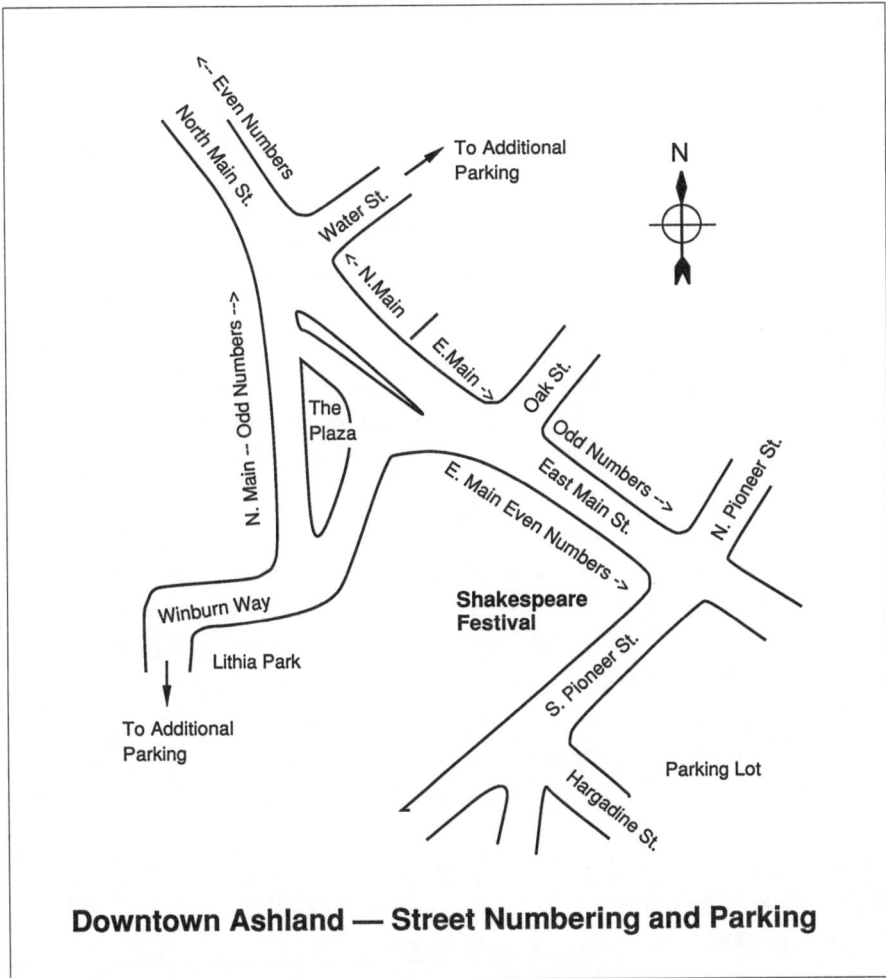

**Downtown Ashland — Street Numbering and Parking**

like 7 North First and 14 South First. It is peculiar to have North Main and North Pioneer less than two blocks apart and nearly perpendicular.

But it is even more peculiar to have 40 North Main and 25 East Main next door to each other on the same side of the street. It happened because the corner that once was there was rounded off to realign the street for smoother traffic flow. The streets don't connect on the other side because the plaza, Lithia Park and Winburn Way come in between, so the switch from odd to even isn't so noticeable.

The other major confusion arises from giving streets which are also highways multiple names like the characters in a Russian novel. North Main St. is also referred to as U.S. 99, Highway 99 N, and as you get into Medford, as South Pacific Highway, and as you continue north, as the Rogue Valley Highway. Ashland St. is also called Ashland Avenue, Highway 66 and Greensprings Highway.

The Chamber of Commerce sells a folding map with a street index and street numbers which is well worth the dollar they charge for it.

**Parking** — Parking downtown is not really the terrible problem that some people would have you believe. Meter maids are busy from 8:30 AM to 8 PM, but there are plenty of spaces where you don't have to risk a ticket. Parking places on the plaza or along Main St. don't stay empty long, but with one or two hour limits, downtown street spaces do turn over. You can't depend on parking right in front of a specific store, but while that may aggravate residents, visitors typically enjoy window shopping and need exercise.

Four hour parking is available along Winburn Way, next to the park and in a lot just beyond the Creek View Cafe. The two level lot off Hargadine also is limited to four hour parking,. (Note that the parking lot across the alley, behind the Mark Antony Hotel, is for hotel guests only.) Four hours is long enough for an afternoon of shopping, or a meal and a play, since the time limit isn't enforced after 8 PM.

All day parking is available in new lots on Water St., just beyond the C St. overpass, and on residential streets, some quite near the shops and theatres.

A few parking spaces are reserved for the handicapped: on Winburn Way near the park entrance (2 spaces), in front of the plaza stores (1), in the lower of the lots off Hargadine (4), and on First Street just above East Main (1).

## WEATHER — AND WHAT TO WEAR

Summer days in Ashland can be very hot — temperatures over 100 degrees are quite common — but the nights are usually comfortably cool. It seems almost worth having a scorching day in order to enjoy the special morning freshness and the balmy evening that go with it. Sudden, brief

A rare storm in 1922 covered the Chautauqua dome with snow and froze the spray of the fountain into cones of ice. *Southern Oregon Historical Society, Evelyn Jurgens Collection*

thunder storms are also part of this weather pattern, and relatively cool, overcast days occur, too.

The easiest way to deal with both the unpredictability of the summer weather and the extreme heat is by dressing in layers, wearing the coolest possible clothing and adding things as needed. Fortunately, Ashland is very informal; there is no place where a woman with bare legs and sandals or a man without a tie and jacket would feel uncomfortable on a hot day.

In winter the cold is less extreme, seldom going far below freezing. In spite of the good skiing in the nearby mountains, snow is infrequent in the valley and doesn't last long. If you plan to ski during the day and return to Ashland at night, you will not need as heavy clothing as you would at typical mountain resorts.

Spring and fall alternate between warm, bright days and cooler, rainy ones. Even when the sun is hot at noon the evenings can be quite chilly. There is a real sense of seasons, a blossomy spring and crisp fall days with colored leaves falling. It rains about twenty inches during the year, so an umbrella may be handy insurance.

A 1910 map designed to promote land sales extols Ashland as a "...climatic paradise...[the] Italy of America..." Hyperbole aside, Ashland's climate really is good for vacationers as well as for the fruit growers they were trying to attract.

Inside the Chautauqua. *Southern Oregon Historical Society*

# You Came For...

Whether it's one of the festivals or some form of outdoor activity that brings you to Southern Oregon, you need to plan well ahead to be sure of getting what you want, when you want it. Many people visit Ashland, especially in the summer months, and demand for tickets and lodgings is high. Increasing numbers of Festival members order Shakespeare tickets in November for the following summer; unusually attractive or inexpensive places to stay are sometimes reserved a year in advance; and though there are many different trips offered by the various rafting companies, only a few people can go on each one. So if you want to float with a particular guide or stay in a special place or get Festival tickets for a specific day, reserve early.

Once you have the basics nailed down, reservations where you're going to stay — lodging is the subject of the next chapter — and arrangements for the main thing you're going to do, you can consider the trimmings. Would you like to take a break from the river to see some plays or hear some music? Would a raft trip wake you up on a day you have no tickets? Would you like to visit a winery, explore the caves, or play tennis? Would your kids enjoy the water slides or a trip to a safari park? How about a day at a quiet lake, or photographing old tombstones, or biking on the back roads, or riding in a hot air balloon?

The possibilities are enormously varied, and for many, all you need to enjoy them is to know they exist. That is true of the museums and old houses and cemeteries you can visit, the natural wonders and scenic places you can explore, the sports facilities you can use. The following sections are about all of these as well as the festival tickets you need to buy months in advance. But since it's almost worse to find out about something a day late than never to have known at all, first are some suggestions for getting current information on what's going to be happening when you're in Ashland. Some are good sources for advance planning, too.

## INFORMATION SOURCES

The best is probably the Ashland Chamber of Commerce where there are huge racks of leaflets to browse through and friendly people to answer questions. In addition to distributing flyers for other organizations, the Chamber puts out some leaflets of its own, notably a calendar of the year's events in Ashland. To obtain a copy of the calendar, or more information about some specific activity, contact them:

*Ashland Chamber of Commerce*              482-3486
*Visitors and Convention Bureau,*
*110 East Main St.*
*P.O. Box 606, Ashland*

Once you are in Ashland you can collect handfuls of literature from the racks in the Chamber's office, next door to the Black Swan Theatre, and, in summer, from the racks at the plaza kiosk, too.

The Medford Visitors and Convention Bureau puts out a similar calendar; in the absence of a Jackson County Tourist Information Office, they include many Jackson County events outside Medford. They will send you a copy, along with masses of other leaflets.

*Medford Chamber of Commerce*        772-5194, 772-6293
*Visitors and Convention Bureau*
*304 S. Central, Medford, 97501*

There's even a statewide calendar of events and exhibits put out by:

*State of Oregon*                    800-547-7842 (USA)
*Economic Development Department*     800-233-3306 (OR)
*Tourism Division*
*Salem, OR 97310*

You can also go to the Park and Recreation Department office for their flyers detailing events in Lithia Park and giving the schedule for the swimming pool and for various other outdoor activities. The office is at the upper end of the park; you go up Winburn Way past the intersection with Granite St. and turn left, across the bridge over Ashland Creek. The office is located in one of the old buildings from the Chautauqua camp and is decorated with photographs that are worth a few minutes to inspect. This is also the place to buy the booklet on the history of Lithia Park.

*City of Ashland*                                                    *488-5340*
*Department of Parks and Recreation*
*340 S. Pioneer St.*
*Open Monday to Friday, 8 AM to Noon and 1 PM to 5 PM*

Information on events sponsored by Southern Oregon State College can be picked up at the Information Office, on Siskiyou Blvd., opposite Andre's Restaurant. Look for the "Visitor Parking" sign as you go south on Siskiyou:

*SOSC Information Office*                                    *482-3311*
*Open Monday to Friday, 8 AM to 5 PM*

The Division of Continuing Education publishes a weekly College Calendar that is principally aimed at students. Although it includes a lot of information only useful to them, it also lists concerts and plays along with wondrous nutty events like Volkswagen stuffing contests that you'd never know about otherwise.

*College Calendar Office*                                    *482-6462*

Sources of information on specific types of college-sponsored events are listed in the sections on that activity — classes, music, theatre, sports or whatever — that follow.

Every Friday the *Ashland Daily Tidings* publishes an entertainment section called "Revels." Besides feature articles and the TV listings, it includes a calendar of the coming week that covers who's entertaining at various nightclubs and restaurants as well as plays, concerts, guided walks, Shakespeare seminars at SOSC and a wide range of other special events. If you come at the wrong time of the week to find one in a news rack, you could try calling the Tidings to see if they still have copies for sale, or you could visit the Library, at the corner of Gresham and Siskiyou. They keep the papers and they have a copier.

The Tidings also publishes a "Shakespeare Supplement" that is full of information; it's usually for sale at the Tudor Guild Shop. The *Medford Mail Tribune* has its own Friday entertainment section called "Tempo" which has possibly more information than "Revels" but lacks the convenient, all on one page calendar. Both papers also distribute a wide ranging supplement on "Southern Oregon Recreation". It is a gold mine of detail about attractions of all sorts, so if you don't see it for sale, contact the papers:

| | |
|---|---|
| *The Ashland Daily Tidings* | *482-3456* |
| *1661 Siskiyou Blvd.* | |
| *The Medford Mail Tribune* | *482-4646* |
| *62 East Main St.* | |

As a last resort, but one that turns up unusual opportunities, look at the posters on telephone poles and bulletin boards. For some events, popular music and dances particularly, this seems to be the major form of publicity.

# ⚜ *Shakespeare*

Of all the varied attractions in Ashland, the Shakespeare Festival is the one that can't be found elsewhere. Other towns have colleges and parks and historic buildings. Other rivers are good for rafting and you can ski on other mountains. But the festival, and the institutions that have grown up around it, such as the Elderhostel programs and the various little theater groups, make Ashland unique.

The Fourth of July, 1935, was the occasion for what founder Angus Bowmer called the First Annual Shakespeare Festival. Everybody has heard the story of how the Chautauqua walls reminded the young instructor of Shakespeare's Globe Theatre. He persuaded the city to support three performances, two of "Twelfth Night" and one of "The Merchant of Venice", in return for sharing the stage with boxing matches intended to cover the plays' deficit. The fights lost money, Shakespeare made enough to pay for both, and the festival is going very strong more than fifty years later.

Of course, it wasn't all that smooth. In the middle of the 1940 season, while Angus Bowmer was on leave of absence, a fire destroyed the costumes and damaged the stage. War was imminent and there was no festival in 1941, or as it turned out, for the rest of the war years.

In 1947 a new stage was built, largely with volunteer labor and donated materials, and the Festival was reopened. In 1959 that stage was replaced with the present one, modeled after the Fortune Theatre, a contemporary of Shakespeare's Globe. The continued success of the Festival made possible the opening of the Angus Bowmer Theatre in 1970 and the Black Swan in 1977. In fact, the Festival needed income from added ticket sales, but the addition of indoor playing spaces changed its character from a summer of amateur fun to a year round, professional operation.

The Festival company started as a mixture of college students and community volunteers. The 1952 program states "The actors are not salaried, although a few of the more experienced are awarded room and board scholarships for the summer." Since then, the festival has gradually become more professional, until today more than half of the actors are

The Festival's second Elizabethan stage as it looked in 1949. *Southern Oregon Historical Society*

Equity members and all are paid. The staff of actors and technical people now numbers close to three hundred and fifty paid professionals. Eight hundred community volunteers still have a vital role off stage; their accomplishments were recently rewarded with a Presidential medal.

Since 1935 the festival has grown from three nights on a makeshift stage, with an audience of 500, to 681 performances in three professionally equipped theatres in 1987, with an audience over 320,000. Starting

24

with two of Shakespeare's most familiar plays, the festival has now produced all of them at least twice. Each year's repertory now includes not only Shakespeare favorites and rarities but also a range of classic and modern plays from other Elizabethan works to world premiers.

If you would like to read more about the history of the festival, two fascinating books are available in the Tudor Guild shop. *As I Remember, Adam* is Angus Bowmer's autobiography; *Golden Fire*, by Edward and Mary Brubaker, details the festival's story with wonderful pictures.

## Seeing Plays

For years, the Festival slogan was "stay four days, see four plays" and for the month of August the repertory rotated every evening in the outdoor theatre. Now the length of the season and the complexity of scheduling in three theatres, two of them available for matinees, has put an end to any such simple formula and made days off essential. The Festival runs from mid February to the end of October, though the outdoor season is limited to the four months with the least rain, and Mondays are dark, with nothing happening on or off stage. The plays are scheduled for performance at different times each week, as much as

Today's Elizabethan Stage with festival dancers and musicians entertaining before the play. *Oregons Shakespearean Festival*

25

overlapping casts will permit, so that someone who can only come on weekends or who works particular evenings can still see them all.

The outdoor Elizabethan Theatre is reserved for Shakespeare and an occasional play by one of his contemporaries. Though the designers work amazing transformations on it, the stage is so specifically Tudor that modern plays would seem unsuited to it. In recent years three plays have alternated here, each playing twice a week. The heat makes matinees impossible for the actors, and probably for the audience too, and the effect of the lighting would be lost. Even night performances in June suffer somewhat from the long twilight.

Nearly thirteen hundred people can attend each outdoor performance. The seats are large and remarkably comfortable considering that they are unpadded metal. 1173 seats are sold, about two thirds of them at the top price, with the rest divided into two less expensive sections at the rear, and 115 standing room places are made available for sold out

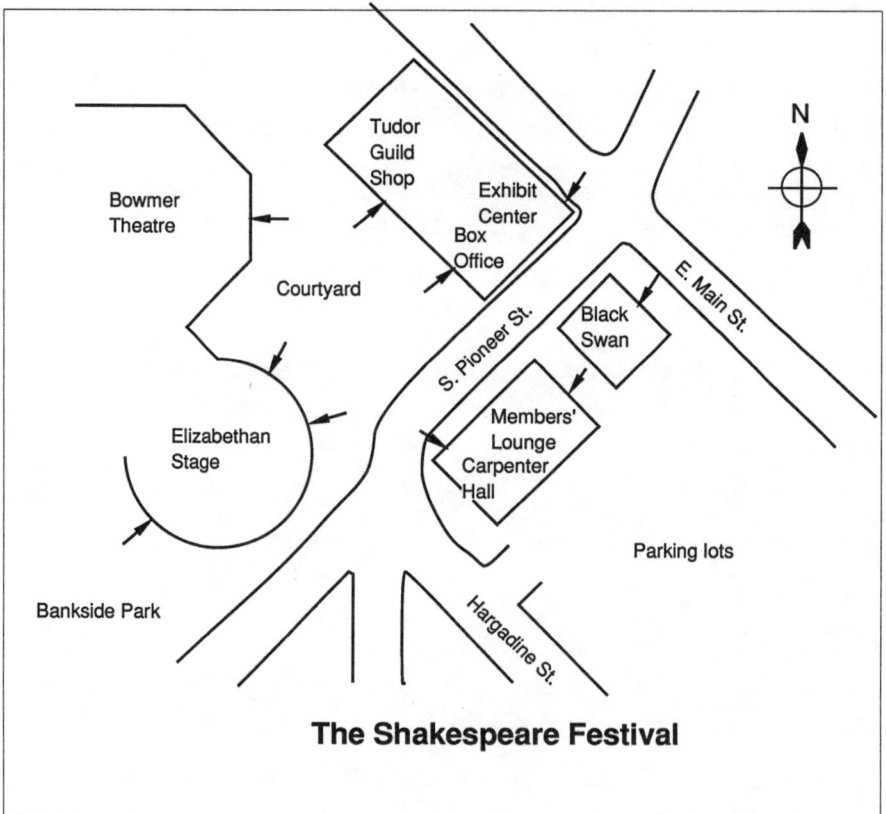

**The Shakespeare Festival**

shows (more than half the performances are sold out). The plays begin precisely at 8:30 PM (8 PM after Labor Day); latecomers risk having to sit at the rear or stand until the intermission.

The Green Shows — the name refers to itinerant musicians performing on the village green, though in Ashland they use the brick courtyard — are designed to get you to the theatres early. At 7 PM (6:30 when the play starts at 8) a procession of costumed musicians and dancers marches out onto the bricks. The style of the dancing and the choice of music are keyed to the evening's outdoor play, perhaps court music before a history or Morris dancing if the play is a rustic comedy.

When the doors open at 7:30 (or 7) this performance is continued on the deck over the control booth, at the rear of the theatre, and ends with the musicians playing on the stage just before the show starts. Also behind the seating area are the restrooms and two booths run by festival volunteer organizations. The Tudor Guild's booth is a miniature of their shop, with a variety of small souvenirs (the ruler ruler, with the kings of England listed on one side and inches on the other, and similar trifles), pamphlets with the stories of the plays, and English toffee and individual pecan pies to munch. The Soroptimists rent blankets and cushions and Beta Sigma Phi members sell coffee and soft drinks from the other. At recently opened stalls at the sides of the theatre wine and champagne are available, hot mulled wine on cold evenings.

The ivy covered walls give the audience some shelter from wind, though it can get chilly, even in summer, and it can rain. Some nights you can sit to the end of the play in short sleeves; on others, bringing or renting a blanket is essential. The vagaries of Ashland weather add a spice of unpredictability to outdoor performances but unless it rains a nonstop deluge, the actors will continue. If the stage is slippery the fights will be slowed way down to avoid skewering anyone. If it's really wet, the costumes will be saved and you'll see Shakespeare in very modern dress. Summer thunder showers are usually brief, but refunds will be given to people who leave because of rain during the first hour and a half of the performance, so save your ticket stub. Unless the performance is canceled, the refund can only be obtained at the time you leave. Lots of hardy folk put on garbage bags and see the play in spite of the rain. According to one veteran actor, it looks from the stage like an audience of cucumbers.

Festival founder Angus Bowmer talking to a group of students. *Oregon Shakespearean Festival*

The Angus Bowmer Theatre is half the size of the outdoor arena, 600 seats and no standees, and has the same price structure for tickets. Starting times and late seating policies are also like those outdoors. The Bowmer is as flexible and modern as the Elizabethan Stage is constrained, with computers controlling the lights and the many movable parts of the stage. This technology has made all kinds of inventive staging possible, from a Restoration comedy whose scenes flashed by on a turntable to "King Lear" set among towering rocks that moved with imperceptible slowness. Four plays are usually running in repertory here, including one by Shakespeare, so the most elaborate sets are designed to be taken down and put up between a matinee and an evening performance. This precisely choreographed frenzy is the subject of one of the videos shown in the Exhibit Center.

The Bowmer lobby is a handsome curved space with a wide view over the Festival courtyard and the town. There are a small souvenir and candy counter and a bar for wine and soft drinks. Displays include photographs of current and past productions, a gorgeous car constructed in the

Festival shops for the 1983 production of "Man and Superman", and the awards the Festival has won. In addition to the President's Volunteer Action Award, there is the Tony (Antoinette Perry Award), the National Governors Association Award and a 50th anniversary resolution from the Oregon Legislature. Plaques with the names of donors to the festival and its endowment are also located here.

The Black Swan is a black box theatre designed for an audience of no more than 150 people. The placement of the seats can be changed each season and the acting space reshaped for each production. As currently configured, there are 138 seats, all priced the same. Originally used for rehearsals and in-company experimental work called Black Swan Projects, it was developed as a public theatre where the actors could work in more intimate contact with their audience. All sorts of shows have been successfully staged here, not just ones with small casts or limited audience appeal; Black Swan tickets are among the most prized at the festival. Because the audience is so close to the actors it is impossible to seat latecomers except at an intermission, and missing the performance won't get you a refund.

The acoustics in all the theatres are excellent — so good in fact that your alarm watch or beeper will be heard by everybody else. Ringing out in a quiet moment in the play, and these do seem to come on the hour, your alarm will be an acute embarrassment to you as well as a distraction to others. And just as you can hear a whisper from the stage, everybody in front of you can hear what you say to your friend in the next seat. For the same reason, clicking cameras and whirring recorders are prohibited by the Festival.

## OTHER ACTIVITIES AND ATTRACTIONS

The Backstage Tour is just that. Members of the acting company and technical staff lead groups through all the theatres, behind the scenes, into the costume shop, past the dressing rooms and out onto the Elizabethan Theatre stage, explaining and answering questions along the way. Tours leave from the Black Swan every morning at 10 AM, except Monday; the tickets are inexpensive and in the summer they tend to sell out in advance.

The Festival Exhibit Center is a museum of festival history and productions. Displays are changed every year and include costumes and props from the previous years' plays, photographs and objects from past productions of the plays in the current repertory, and panels on actors and directors who have gone on from Ashland to become famous. There is a room with old costumes to try on — a volunteer will snap your picture — and several videos about the festival and Ashland to watch. Admission is included with backstage tour tickets or is available separately, for a minimal amount.

Festival Noons are a series of varied, hour-long activities at noon-time in the summer months. A leaflet called "Summer Pleasures" details them, and weekly schedules are also available from the box office. There are lectures twice a week and occasional concerts in Carpenter Hall; tickets are required, though the price is nominal. The annual concert in which the festival dancers kick off their Renaissance personas and dance in every other style gets better every year. Hidden underneath the ruffs and pantaloons of the Green Shows are belly dancers and ballerinas and great comic talents.

Every noon when there is not a lecture or a concert, except Mondays, when the whole Festival takes a day off, there will be a talk by an actor or other festival staff person in Bankside Park, just on the other side of the Elizabethan Theatre from the courtyard. These are informal, question and answer sessions and are free. You learn all kinds of arcane facts, get insights into the creative process and have a little fun. For example, Associate Director Pat Patton described the joys of staging Sam Shepard's "Curse of the Starving Class" with a live lamb in it. Replacement lambs are needed as they quickly grow too big to be carried. They bleat or pee, try to climb out of their pen or fall over and play dead, anything to distract the actors and the audience. The lambs also get pet names: Cybill Sheepherd, Ewe Two, Meryl Sheep, Sam Sheepard. It's fun to feel part of the family and the Parktalks help make that connection.

In September, there are Festival Forums in Carpenter Hall, continuing in the noon format with panels of company members discussing and answering questions about their work. There are also play readings, a new program designed to introduce both audience and company to new works.

## SPECIAL EVENTS

The opening of the summer season is celebrated with a buffet dinner and entertainment by festival musicians and dancers in Lithia Park preceding the opening of the first play in the Elizabethan Theatre. Called the Feast of the Tribe of Will, it has become a much loved tradition. There are also two Renaissance Feasts with period music and dancing that are held in early July on the SOSC campus. The renaissance food is made from recipes in Madge Lorwin's *Dining With Shakespeare* and includes dishes like Soused Carrots, Apples Stewed in Ambergris, Fermenty of Red Wheat and Chewets of Veal. These events are scheduled well in advance so that tickets can be ordered at the same time as your play tickets.

On a few summer Mondays the Elizabethan Theatre is the site of concerts or other performances. The Duck's Breath Mystery Theatre has appeared here for several years and there have been chamber orchestra and brass ensemble concerts. These events are not scheduled much in advance so you almost have to leave catching them to luck. They are listed in the Summer Pleasures leaflet.

Finally, the closing of the summer season is celebrated with a brief Candlelight Ceremony following the last outdoor performance.

## MEMBERSHIP

Festival membership comes with spectacular benefits, over and above feeling good about supporting a good institution. Memberships begin at $25 for students and retired people and $35 for everyone else, and go up in steps, with added benefits for more generous contributions. Members get the first choice of tickets during a three month presale period; those who give $250 or more enjoy a two week head start when only their orders are filled. Throughout the year members' orders are processed first on the day they arrive.

Members pay twenty per cent less for performances in February, March, April, May, September and October. They can buy tickets to preview performances in the Bowmer and Elizabethan Theatres for half the price of a regular performance, which also amounts to a twenty per cent discount from non-member prices. They receive a 10% discount on purchases over $10 at the Tudor Guild Shop. They and their guests can visit the Exhibit Center without charge.

31

There is a members' lounge in Carpenter Hall, with comfortable sofas and chairs and uncrowded restrooms. Coffee, wine and soft drinks are available at modest prices. Wine and cheese receptions with the actors are held there after summer matinees.

With larger gifts come added benefits in addition to the two weeks of early presale. Such things as free backstage tour tickets, invitations to opening night parties, complementary play tickets and gifts of merchandise are offered to encourage generosity. Give $5000 and a cast party will be given just for you!

## GETTING TICKETS

Arriving at the Shakespeare Box Office on the day of the play you want to see is much riskier than arriving in town without a room reserved. There's always another motel a little farther out of town, but the theatres are finite and performances are often sold out long in advance. If it's a summer weekend and the play is a popular one or is showing in the Black Swan, your chances of seeing it will be slim indeed.

The season schedule is announced in the fall of the preceding year and order forms are mailed to a huge number of members, ticket buyers and

### 1988 TICKET PRICES

Elizabethan and Bowmer Theatres

| | | | |
|---|---|---|---|
| Regular Performances | $18.00 | 14.00 | 10.00 |
| Previews | 12.60 | 9.80 | 7.00 |
| Children | 9.00 | 7.00 | 5.00 |
| Members (low season) | 14.40 | 11.20 | 8.00 |
| Members Previews | 9.00 | 7.00 | 5.00 |

Black Swan

| | |
|---|---|
| Regular Performances | 18.00 |
| Previews | 12.60 |
| Children | 9.00 |
| Members (low season) | 14.40 |

| | | |
|---|---|---|
| Backstage Tours | 6.00 | }  *Children's tickets half price* |
| Festival Noons | 3.00 | |
| Exhibit Center | 1.00 | |

others. A card or call to the box office will put your name on the list. Members' orders are processed first during a presale period, roughly November through January. Orders from non-members are filed in the order received and processed as soon as the member presale period is over. Orders can be placed by mail or by telephone:

OSFA Box Office                                503-482-4331

Box 158, Ashland, Or 97520.

Starting with the members' presale period, telephone orders can be made weekdays from 9:30 AM to 5 PM. After the season opens in February, the box office can be telephoned on performance days up until the time the play starts (8 PM, 8:30 from the opening of the Elizabethan Theatre to Labor Day). The box office windows, in the festival courtyard, are also open once the season is underway, from 10 AM until play time, or until 5 PM on days with no performance.

Ticket sales are final. The box office will exchange tickets that they receive at least seven days before the performance, with a $1 per ticket charge that is waived for members. Only members may return tickets for a refund; receipt by the box office a minimum of seven days in advance and a $1 per ticket fee are required. Others may donate their excess tickets back to the Festival and claim their cost as a charitable deduction on their income tax returns. There are no exchanges or refunds on bargain package tickets. Unwanted tickets are seldom a problem if you're going to be in Ashland; there is a lively market (at the original price — I've never seen any scalping) in the Festival courtyard.

In addition to special prices available to members, three bargain ticket packages are offered to everyone. Each gives you the best top price seats available at the time you order at one third off. The Theatre Lovers Spectacular is tickets to all eleven productions. The Mini Spectacular is seven or more plays on any Sunday through Thursday. The Bowmer Bonanza is four productions in the Angus Bowmer Theatre on any Sunday through Thursday. These packages are available all during the season except July and August.

There are three other sources of bargain price tickets. Tickets for preview performances cost thirty per cent less than the regular price. Also, the box office may declare that a performance has so many unsold tickets that seats will be sold at half price; these are called "rush" tickets, though they are reserved seats, and are available to members after 11 AM

Would-be audience sitting on the courtyard bricks, waiting at the box office for returned tickets. *Oregon Shakespearean Festival*

on the day of the show and to seniors and students with I.D. one hour before the performance. And last, during the spring and fall there are bargain matinees for student groups and retired people; excess tickets for these performances are sometimes available from the box office.

If you haven't been able to get tickets in advance, there are several ways to proceed. If your membership entitles you to it, get on the waiting list. It is hard to predict how effective this will be, but it can't hurt. Any tickets turned back by 6:30 PM the night before the performance will go first to wait-listed members.

At 10 AM on the day of the performance the box office hands out priority numbers, though the line to get them sometimes starts forming early in the morning. Each person in line can get a maximum of two numbers for a show and each number entitles the holder to buy two tickets. If there are any tickets turned back that day they will be sold to the holders of these numbers at 1 PM for matinees and 6 PM for evening shows. Reserved tickets that are not picked up are sold fifteen minutes before the play starts, so it's worth checking back then. And you can always stand on the bricks with a sign and a hopeful expression; maybe you'll be lucky.

## BRINGING CHILDREN

Children younger than three are not admitted to the theatres. For children between ages three and eleven most festival tickets are half price, but it's a rare three year old that can sit quietly through a whole play. Even very young children enjoy sitting on the grass and watching the singing and dancing of the Green Show, and nobody minds if they aren't perfectly quiet there. After that it may be best to park the very young with one of the Tudor Guild's list of qualified baby sitters so that the rest of the family can enjoy the play.

Slightly older children, and only you know if yours have reached this stage, will be fascinated by the backstage tour and the dress-up room in the exhibit center, and with some preparation, can really enjoy a Shakespeare comedy. Lambs' *Tales From Shakespeare* is the classic book to read to children, but there are a number of more modern books of Shakespeare stories. Bernard Miles has written two volumes, each with the stories of five plays and big, colorful illustrations by Victor Ambrus that appeal to younger children. In a pinch, the booklet put out each year by the festival can help, though its tone is adult and analytical and quite misses out on the poetry and atmosphere that the Lambs and Miles both capture so well.

Young people who start out loving "As You Like It" and "A Midsummer Night's Dream" go on to enjoy "Romeo and Juliet" and "Macbeth" and eventually appreciate the history plays, though enjoying them requires being old enough to understand a little English history. Older children can also get great pleasure from many of the non-Shakespearean plays put on at the Festival, but which ones is sometimes hard to tell from the Festival brochures. The descriptions are intended to guide adults' choices and barely hint at violence, sex, nudity, or crude language, let alone the possibility of boring a child. By the time your children pay full price they'll be taking in the whole repertory and you'll think fondly of how cheap babysitting was.

## HANDICAPPED ACCESS

Wheelchair seating is available in all three theatres, but the box office needs to be informed at the time tickets are ordered. In the Bowmer and Black Swan there are two wheelchair spaces that are made by removing seats which would otherwise be sold. The Bowmer seats are in the top price section. In the Elizabethan Theatre, a wooden platform is used to make a level parking space on the ramp at the end of a row of seats. These can be placed at either the front, at the top price, or rear, at the lowest price. There is also enough space between the rows of outdoor seats to accommodate a wheelchair if you can switch to a regular seat for the performance, but you have to arrange to be let into the theatre before anyone else is seated for this to work.

The box office people will try to accommodate any other special seating needs. For example, they are happy to arrange for seats as close to the stage as possible for patrons with impaired hearing or vision, if they are asked. Infrared hearing devices are available for rent in both the Elizabethan and Bowmer theatres.

## COMING IN GROUPS

Special prices and activities are available to groups of fifteen or more. These can be previously existing organizations, friends who choose to vacation together, or a group put together by a travel agent. Groups of students and retired persons can take advantage of some special benefits offered only to them. For information and booking for groups call:

*Group Bookings*                               *482-2111, ext. 255.*

Currently any group is given twenty per cent off the price of tickets for regular midweek performances, except in July and August. Student and senior groups receive a discount for most weekend performances, as well. Travel agents and tour operators are given discounts all year because they help the festival to reach patrons who wouldn't otherwise come.

Seniors and students are also offered the special matinee performances and ticket packages at half price or less. The Quartet is a bargain matinee plus three other midweek plays and the Trio is three plays on the same terms. The Daily Double is two plays on one day, in the Elizabethan or Bowmer Theatres. As the airlines always say, other restrictions apply, so a close reading of the special group brochure is essential before placing

The courtyard at the center of the Shakespeare Festival with the Elizabethan and Bowmer Theatres; the box office and Tudor Guild Shop are out of the picture to the right. *Oregon Shakespearean Festival, Hank Kranzler.*

a group order. One bonus for anyone planning to bring a group of high-school age and younger students: one free ticket for an adult chaperone comes with each twenty student tickets purchased.

In the spring and fall several kinds of activities are available to enhance your group's enjoyment of the plays. Two hour workshops on acting, or on dealing with Shakespeare's verse, are led by two Festival actors. Discussions are an hour's conversation with one member of the company on similar subjects. Both of these are scheduled in the morning and early Backstage Tours may be arranged in conjunction with them. Warm-ups are half-hour preparation sessions given by a Festival staff person shortly before the play begins. They're aimed at alerting possibly inexperienced playgoers to things they should look for as the play progresses. There is a charge for all these group activities and they need to be scheduled at the time the tickets are ordered. Groups can also schedule a special time to visit the Exhibit Center.

In addition to these programs, informal question and answer sessions with the cast follow the bargain matinees; audience members gather in the Bowmer lobby, dragging the benches together and sitting on the carpet, and as the actors get cleaned up, they join them for what can be very revealing discussions.

If you are interested in coming to the Festival as part of a group and can't find fourteen friends, groups are sometimes organized by college drama departments or as university extensions classes. If you're old enough you could try the Elderhostel program described in the next section, and travel agents and tour operators are another source.

If you can't find any locally organized tours, Southern Oregon Reservation Center sells packages of two or more nights in a motel or bed and breakfast and tickets to two or more plays, but without transportation or the companionship of a group. Commercial tours and packages are convenient but not necessarily economical when compared with the same lodging and tickets bought directly, at individual rates.

*Southern Oregon Reservation Center*           *488-1011*
*1-800-547-8052 (USA)*
*1-800-533-1311 (OR)*

# *More Entertainment*

Don't despair if you can't get all the Shakespeare Festival tickets you hoped for. There is so much good theatre in Ashland that it would really be sensible to plan free evenings during your vacation on which to see whatever else is playing. There is also a whole summer of outdoor music at the Britt Festivals in Jacksonville and a variety of other music and dance throughout the year

## THEATRE

You might think that one huge festival was more than enough theatre for a town of fifteen thousand people, but several small theatre companies also thrive here, relying on the pool of theatrical talent and the audience drawn to Ashland by the Shakespeare Festival. They put on plays intermittently and on no predictable schedule, but the level of professionalism is high and taking in whatever happens to be playing when you have a free night is likely to result in an enjoyable evening. Look for productions by:

*The Actor's Workshop*                                          *482-9659*
*295 East Main St., #5*

Their space is tiny; it takes a shoehorn to fit the 42 people they admit each night and in the front row your feet are on the stage. None-the-less, the designers make ingenious and entertaining sets in this cramped room. In the five years since the company's founding by Alison Grant and Michael O'Rourke, over 30 different shows have been staged with local casts, including some played entirely by children. While the Festival was playing Sam Shepard's "Curse of the Starving Class" the Workshop did his "True West" and they've done a range of other plays from Christmas one-acts to "The Lewis and Clark Expedition."

*Ashland Children's Theatre*                                   482-9870
*31 Gresham St.*

Dorothy Potter and her casts of elementary and high school students have produced several musicals aimed at young audiences. ACT is as much a school as a theatre company and Ms. Potter's aim is to create an opportunity for interested young people to become involved in theatre without pressure or competition. Now, with space in the Performing Arts Center being developed in the old armory, she hopes to add classes in the technical aspects of theatre and with them, more opportunities for children who are not performers. If you're traveling with young children, an ACT production might be a welcome change.

*Ashland Resident Theatre*                                    482-4292

According to the **Tidings** reviewer, this is one of the oldest of Ashland's little theatres. They produced Caryl Churchill's "Top Girls" in 1986 in association with several departments at SOSC including Women's Studies. In 1987 the theatre was active in Seattle; plans for future productions in Ashland have not been announced.

*Coyote Radio*
*Butler Band shell, Lithia Park*

Ashland's answer to "The Prairie Home Companion" is a variety show of local talent that appeared on several Sunday evenings in July and August, 1987. It isn't on the radio yet, in spite of the name, but the quality of the local talent here makes it worth watching the various calendars and bulletin boards to catch the next live performance.

*Emmaus Theatre Company*
*5301 Highway 66, near Emigrant Lake*

A free passion play has been presented here on Easter Sunday; before planning to attend you should check the Tidings to see if it is being repeated.

*Lyric Theatre Company*                                       488-1926
*162 N. Pioneer St.*

The artistic director and star of this relatively new venture is Joe Vincent, a veteran of many Shakespeare Festival seasons. The Lyric's first production was "Stop The World — I Want To Get Off." They have also done "Jacques Brel Is Alive and Well and Living in Paris" and in 1987 they took "The Fantasticks" to Medford and Grants Pass as well as Ashland. The Lyric Theatre's aim is to produce full-scale musicals in Ashland — they've been done successfully at the Britt Festivals and by Rogue Music Theatre in Grants Pass — and their efforts have been well received.

### Mixed Company 488-2780
### P.O. Box 1364, Ashland

Mixed Company is the brainchild of Dori Appel and Carolyn Myers, both of whom write, act and direct. They have produced both their own plays and some by other authors, concentrating on plays that touch on women's issues and contemporary relationships and emphasizing humor and entertainment, not preaching. Their "Female Troubles" was selected for the National Festival of Women's Theatre and they have also brought productions to several colleges and conferences. Mixed Company doesn't have a permanent space; most recently they did "Gertrude Stein and a Companion" at Positively Fourth Street.

### New Playwright's Theatre 482-9236
### 31 Water St., underneath the Lithia Creek Arts Gallery

According to an article in the Tidings in January, 1987, NPT had produced over fifty plays in its five years of existence, most of them new scripts. Founded by Bradford O'Neil and Ruth Wire, and still under O'Neil's leadership, the company currently puts on a season of about seven plays in the spring and summer. O'Neil directs many of the plays and writes at least one new one for each season as well; he's written more than twenty so far. A recent first was "Vacancy," which is about an Asian immigrant; it was produced with an all Equity cast with support from the Association of Asian Pacific American Artists. NPT has also staged a number of well known plays, including "Educating Rita" and Jean Genet's "The Maids." Unusual adventures in theatre are possible in the theatre's new basement home.

### Oregon Cabaret Theatre 488-2902
### First and Hargadine Sts.
### P.O. Box 1149, Ashland

Preservationists and architecture buffs should come here just to applaud the creative recycling of a 1911 church that stood empty for years. The format of Cabaret productions is musical revue with food served beforehand, both for full-length evening performances and hour-long midnight shows. Generous hors d'oeuvres plates and desserts are served, along with beer, wine, coffee and fruit juice. The Cabaret has been an immediate success, selling out and extending runs of justly popular productions such as "A. . . My Name is Alice," a feminist review, and "Quilters," based on the writings and oral histories of pioneer women.

*The Quartz Theatre*        *482-8119*
*2500 Siskiyou Blvd.*

Seeing a production in this little room where the cast may outnumber the audience has the quality of being let in on a secret. Robert Spira, the presiding genius, writes half the plays and conducts a nationwide search for new plays for the other half of his season. He looks for the writer whose ideas and poetic voice are worth developing, who can become the next Shakespeare. For his own plays he writes music, directs and produces, and serves coffee and brownies at intermission, talking to his audience the while. Both space and budget limit what he can do, particularly with sets and costumes, but his plays are worth experiencing.

*Southern Oregon State College*
*Department of Theatre Arts*        *482-6346*
*Box Office*        *482-6348*

SOSC is a designated center of excellence for arts training in the Oregon state college and university system and the only Oregon school to grant a bachelor of fine arts in theatre. The $3.8 million Theatre Arts complex was completed in 1980 and includes the Dorothy Stolp Theatre, a thrust stage and auditorium seating 327 and the Center Square, a black box theatre for 80 to 100 playgoers. The college season usually includes four productions, the first of which is dinner theatre in a cabaret setting on the huge Dorothy Stolp stage. Nearly half of SOSC's students are 30 or older and the program is conceived as pre-professional training. Students also work on the design and production of sets and costumes, and the budget allows for quality only surpassed at the Shakespeare Festival. Their production of "Cloud Nine" won a regional award in the American College Theatre Festival.

## MOVIES

*Varsity Theater*                                          *482-3321*
*166 E. Main St.*

The original theater has been divided into three sections and a fourth space, called the Backstage, has been created at the rear of the building. More than one film is shown each day in some of them, so that you have lots of choices here. Their Tightwad Tuesday special is admission for $1.50, and it draws a crowd. The Backstage is also sometimes used for live productions by one or another of the little theatre companies.

In summer the Ashland Public Library shows silent films in the Lithia Park band shell. The Park and Recreation Department flyer lists the dates, or you can check the calendar in the Friday *Tidings*.

On Sundays Jazmin's has "Free Flicks" with free popcorn and there are Midnight Munchie Movies on Fridays and Saturdays at The Bushes. Call for program information:

*Jazmin's*                                                 *488-0883*
*The Bushes*                                               *482-3853*

## DANCE

The State Ballet of Oregon performs on Monday evenings in summer, at 7:30, in the Lithia Park band shell. The programs, which change each month, are sponsored by the park department and are free. In the past the ballet staged winter performances and hopes to again. For information, call the Park Department or:

*State Ballet of Oregon*                                   *482-4789*

For the kind of dance that you do rather than watch, look in the "Revels" calendar. Folk dancing evenings at the Community Center on Winburn Way and at the Plaza Dance Studio are announced there, as are the dances held at Positively Fourth Street. There is also dancing at Jazmin's, depending on the kind of music being played, and on weekends there is a small combo at the Ashland Hills' Cascade Lounge. Or there are steak BBQ's with square dancing at the Box R Ranch; call for the schedule and to make the necessary reservations:

*Box R Ranch*                                              *482-1873*
*6799 Hwy 66*

## Classical Music

Much of the musical activity in Ashland is connected with the college. The Division of Continuing Education sponsors visiting recitalists and chamber groups who appear in the handsome concert hall on the campus. There's nothing small-town about these performances except the enthusiastic turn out of local people. So many tickets were sold for a recent concert by a visiting Russian pianist that extra chairs had to be squeezed into the aisles and set up on stage. For information or tickets, contact:

| | |
|---|---|
| *Continuing Education* | *482-6331* |
| *Music Department* | *482-6101* |

There are also locally produced operas and a season of symphony concerts.

| | |
|---|---|
| *Rogue Opera* | *482-6400* |
| *Southern Oregon State College* | |

Supporting three opera productions each year is quite an achievement for a small town. Rogue Opera imports some talent for its big fall production and uses local singers and students in the spring. The Rogue Valley Symphony serves as the orchestra. At Christmas a local production is aimed at children. One year it was a one hour, eight singer version of "The Magic Flute" that toured four southern Oregon cities in addition to playing in Ashland.

| | |
|---|---|
| *Rogue Valley Symphony* | *482-6353* |
| *Southern Oregon State College* | |

The symphony is not a full-time professional orchestra, but it draws on Ashland's unusually rich resources of talent and is warmly supported by the community. Its members include professional musicians, students earning college credit, and community people. Performances of each of the five subscription concerts are given in Medford and Grants Pass as well as Ashland; the Ashland series sells out, though returned tickets are often available. The orchestra sponsors a west coast competition for a young soloist to perform with it, gives concerts for local school districts, and does occasional special programs, too.

The Park and Recreation Department sponsors weekly band concerts in summer, at the Lithia Park band shell, where you can sit on the lawn and picnic. They play every Thursday at 7:30 PM and at noon on July 4th.

The band has about seventy five members and is supported by the city; their concerts are broadcast over local public radio.

## POPULAR MUSIC

There are two places in Ashland to hear jazz, rock, and all the other contemporary forms of popular music:

*Jazmin's*                                              *488-0883*
*180 C St.*

A restaurant and bar with varied musical groups appearing most evenings of the week.

*Positively Fourth Street*                              *482-9401*
*265 4th St., in the railroad district*

A performance space that is intermittently used for plays, music and dances.

A concert in the Lithia Park bandshell. *Ashland Chamber of Commerce, photo Kevin Carpenter*

45

At SOSC, summer beer gardens with entertainment take place at the Stevenson Student Union and there are occasional concerts, too. There is also sometimes live entertainment in bars and restaurants, at the Ashland Hills Inn, Alex's and the Mark Antony, among others.

## THE PETER BRITT FESTIVALS

The Britt Festivals celebrated their twenty-fifth anniversary in 1987, and like the Shakespeare Festival, they have grown, from two weeks of classical music to five festivals covering the whole summer and the whole range of music and dance. The classical music festival in August is still the largest, but there is now a musical theatre festival in June and early July and festivals of bluegrass, jazz and dance with concerts throughout the summer.

Peter Britt was a Swiss photographer who came to the United States in 1845 and to Jacksonville in 1852, where he settled and worked, for the rest of his life. Britt and his children were also avid horticulturists, growing many sub-tropical plants in the garden around their house. The last of the children died in 1954, and the house burned soon after, but the festivals are held in the garden which was left to Southern Oregon State College and subsequently transferred to the Jackson County Park system.

The Festival grounds lie on the hillside, just above the old town. There is parking in a lot across the highway, from which there is a lighted path through the old garden area where a few of Britt's fruit trees are still growing. If you park in the town a cable car shuttle will take you up the hill, though it's not a long walk.

The buildings, which recently won an architectural award for the designer, Gary Afseth, are redwood, at once contemporary and rustic. The patterned shingles on the steep, overhanging roofs may remind you of Victorian houses, or perhaps the wooden folk architecture of Norway.

To celebrate the twenty-fifth anniversary six hundred substantial wooden benches were installed, making it possible for the first time to sell reserved seats, though general admission, for seating on the hillside, is still available. Picnicking is a tradition here, with many of the concerts beginning as early as 6:30 PM. Concession booths, mostly operated by the volunteers of the Britt Society, sell wine, beer, burgers and hot dogs, ice cream, and more elegant, catered food, too. There are handsome new picnic tables, matching the new seats, scattered under the oak trees; groups of eight or more can reserve them.

The orchestra for the classical festival is comprised of paid professionals who come from all over the country. Part of the volunteer tradition, which is as strong here as at the Shakespeare Festival, involves housing the musicians with local families, some of whom have boarded the same player each summer for years. There is also a group of orchestra members who camp with their families on the Applegate River.

A Peter Britt photograph of his own home and garden. *Southern Oregon Historical Society*

For the music theatre festival a production of "Grease" was organized from local talent and other productions have been brought in by touring companies. The dance concerts are given by well known companies, and the jazz and bluegrass concerts are also by touring performers. Their availability dictates the somewhat scattered schedule for these festivals.

As at the Shakespeare Festival, Britt Festival membership gives the contributor priority in ordering reserved seats, but the reward for generosity is a choice of free tickets or discount coupons, the number depending on the size of the donation made. Discounts are also offered for children (with no lower age limit), students and seniors, and for groups. An Early Ticket Buyer Bonus gives you four seats for the price of three if you order before June 1st; the Classical Concert Lover's Special is six general admissions to the classical festival at a substantial saving; and there are also discount packages for jazz festival tickets.

The schedule for the Britt concerts comes out in the spring, by which time you may well have ordered Shakespeare tickets. However, there are concerts in all the festivals on Monday evenings, when the Shakespeare Festival is closed. There is also classical music on Sunday mornings and a special family concert on a Saturday morning, which will work if you don't have a matinee in Ashland that same day.

To obtain a brochure or order tickets, contact the festivals:

*Peter Britt Festivals*               773-6077
*P.O. Box 1124*                  *1-800-882-7488 (USA)*
*45 N. Front St.*                 *1-800-332-7488 (OR)*
*Medford, OR 97501*              *779-0847 (group orders)*
*The box office is open 9 AM to 6 PM starting in May.*

## OTHER ENTERTAINMENT OUTSIDE ASHLAND

*Barnstormers Little Theatre*               479-3557
*112 N.E. Evelyn St., Grants Pass*
A long established amateur theatre.

*Broadway's Best*                      776-2770
*Harry and David's Restaurant*
*2836 S. Pacific Highway, Medford*
Dinner with a cabaret show on summer weekends.

*Medford Civic Ballet*                 772-1362

*Medford Civic Community Theatre*      772-6964

*Medford Community Concerts*           773-5992

*The Minshall Theatre*                 535-5250
*101 Talent Ave., Talent*

Old fashioned hiss-the-villain melodrama and gay nineties revue in the summer, and sometimes other productions during the rest of the year.

*Rogue Music Theatre*                                    *479-5541*
*Rogue Community College*
*3345 Redwood Highway, Grants Pass*
Classic Broadway musicals staged outdoors.

Live entertainment is also available at restaurants in Medford:
   *The Red Lion Inn*                                    *779-5811*
   *Nendel's Motor Inn*                                  *779-3141*
   *Digger O'Dell's Restaurant*                          *779-6100*
   *Sunday's Restaurant*                                 *770-4905*
Browsing through the *Medford Tribune* may yield other possibilities.

The Elizabethan Stagehouse, dimensioned after the stages of the Henslowe and Alleyn-Peter Street contract for the Fortune Theatre of Shakespeare's London, 1599. *Oregon Shakespearean Festival*

# Education

## THE FESTIVAL INSTITUTE

Each summer the Festival Institute offers a series of classes for teachers, high school students and the play-going public. For more information or to register, contact:

*Oregon Shakespearean Festival Institute*    *482-2111, ext. 244.*

Wake Up With Shakespeare includes seeing seven plays, a Shakespeare film and the week's noon programs. Participants also join in four sessions of discussion and preparation, lead by company members and festival staff, and a backstage tour. These classes run from Monday to Saturday every week from early in July to late in August. They are intended for people of all ages and all levels of play-going experience.

The Festival Round Table on Plays and Productions, which is given once each summer in late June, is a more scholarly examination of all nine plays in the repertory at that time. The session lasts for ten days and involves lively discussion in classes with company members and visiting scholars every morning. Included are tickets for all the plays, the Festival Noons, the Backstage Tour and the Renaissance Feast. College credit is available.

For teachers there are: Shakespeare Athletics (athletic minds, not bodies), two intensive weeks on teaching Shakespeare as theatre that includes seeing all the plays; Athletics Reunion, a one week refresher that includes a rafting trip as well as plays and classes; and Directors Forum, a week concerned with directing student productions. Graduate level credit is available.

For students there is the Summer Seminar for High School Juniors. Since relatively small numbers of students can participate, the festival looks for energetic and creative young people whose enthusiasm for what they learn in Ashland will be communicated to other students when they return to school in the fall. Applications with recommendations from teachers and other adults are required. The seminar lasts two weeks in early August and exposes the students to all facets of festival operations. In addition to seeing plays, they take acting workshops and join in discussions with technical staff people and take part in a meeting of a mock school board, played by the festival Board of Directors, where students have to defend their school's drama program against budget cuts. It is an intensive program.

Southern Oregon State Normal School circa 1909. *Ashland Public Library, Evelyn Jurgens Collection, print by Terry Skibby*

## SOUTHERN OREGON STATE COLLEGE

Southern Oregon State sponsors a surprising variety of programs that short-term visitors can take advantage of. The usual college fare of visiting lecturers, films, exhibits and concerts can be discovered through the college and student union information offices and the various departments.

| | |
|---|---|
| *SOSC Information Office* | *482-3311* |
| *Activities Office* | *482-7151* |
| *Student Union Information* | *482-6464* |

| | |
|---|---|
| *Department of Theatre Arts Box Office* | *482-6348* |
| *Department of Music* | *482-6101* |
| *Division of Continuing Education* | *482-6331* |

In addition to these and to the Shakespeare Festival Institute programs, to which the college contributes its facilities and occasionally members of its staff, there are:

Summer Seminars, put on by the Shakespearean Studies Program, a joint effort of the English Department and the Division of Continuing Education. Each is a two hour session devoted to a single play in the festival repertory. Shakespearean Studies also sponsors a summer institute for high school teachers. For dates and times, or for a schedule of all the other continuing education programs, some of which are single events or weekend workshops that a visitor could participate in, contact the Division of Continuing Education.

In 1987, Shakespearean Studies sponsored a monthly series of programs in the Ashland, Medford and Grants Pass public libraries called Living with Shakespeare and focused on seven plays corresponding to the seven ages of man. The Ashland Library is another creation of the town's active, turn-of-the-century women and it is still a center of local educational activities For information on future programs, contact:

| | |
|---|---|
| *The Ashland Public Library* | *482-1151* |
| *At the corner of Gresham St. and Siskiyou Blvd.* | |

The Britt Summer Arts Training Institute is jointly sponsored by the College and the Britt Festivals. Intensive workshops in jazz, bluegrass, folk and modern dancing, chamber music and youth orchestra were put on for the twenty-fifth anniversary season and the intention is to continue to expand this kind of activity. The Britt Festivals brochure will include information on some upcoming workshops and others will be publicized as they are arranged; for details, call or write:

| | |
|---|---|
| *Peter Britt Festivals* | *779-0847* |
| *P.O. Box 1124, Medford, OR 97501* | |

## ELDERHOSTEL

Elderhostel is a world-wide program of non-credit college courses for people aged sixty and over, and their spouses or companions no younger than fifty. The typical program involves a week at a college, staying in the dorms and eating with the students. Hostelers take up to three classes and participate in a variety of extracurricular activities as well. The 1987 price was $215 per person plus the cost of tickets to the plays, surely a bargain.

Ashland Elderhostel has grown to be one of the largest programs in part because seeing plays  and taking a class about them is included in most of the sessions. The variety of other subjects available to the hostelers is amazing; a recent brochure offered American History Through Folk Music, What's All the Fuss About Wines, Tai Chi - The Chinese Way of Exercise, Demystifying the Mushroom, Modern French Theatre, Fine Arts and the Italian Renaissance, The Golden Age of Polyphony - Music of the Renaissance, Folk Dancing of the Balkans, and many more.

For a world-wide listing of Elderhostel programs, write to:

*Elderhostel*
*80 Boylston St., Suite 400*
*Boston, MA 02116*

For more information on Elderhostel programs in Oregon, contact:

*Elderhostel State Office*                  *1-800-232-9653, ext. 435*
*Administration Building 305*                  *838-1220, ext. 435*
*Western Oregon State College*
*Monmouth, OR 97361*

Senior Ventures is Southern Oregon State College's own program for Elderhostel graduates and others age 55 and over. There are both overseas travel programs, as there are with Elderhostel, and classes in Ashland that include the festival plays. The contact for further information about Senior Ventures programs is:

*Senior Ventures*                  *503-482-6378*
*Southern Oregon State College*
*Siskiyou Center for Continuing Education*

Lectures and Lunches is a special program of the Division of Continuing Education in which local residents can take the Elderhostel classes while living at home. People who are physically unable to cope with the student accommodations can also participate this way. However, the communal spirit of the Elderhostel groups is one of their major assets; if you stay in a motel you miss much of that, and too many people doing so would dilute the group spirit for everyone. For this reason only visitors with health problems, such as the need for a special diet or a private bathroom, are admitted to this program which is otherwise reserved for those who live within commuting distance.

Handicapped visitors should ask about the accessibility of any campus event or facility before coming. SOSC is located on rather hilly ground and some of the paths are steep; in addition, they have made relatively little progress in providing wheelchair access to campus buildings. Only a few of the buildings used in the Elderhostel programs have elevators or wheelchair lifts, so it's vital to inform the Elderhostel office of any physical limitations as soon as possible.

## MUSEUMS

Southern Oregon State College is also the site of several museums and art galleries that can provide an hour's entertainment away from the crowds and the shops. They are:

*Schneider Museum of Art*                                  482-6245
*On Indiana St., just off Siskiyou Blvd.*
*Open Tuesday to Friday 11 AM to 5 PM, Saturday 1 PM to 5 PM*

The building is a delight in itself. As you enter, notice how the linear metal sculpture has been used to balance the facade and how the pattern of the door grille echoes the shape of the windows above it. The Schneiders' collection, principally the work of their friend Waldo Peirce, is housed here and there is one large gallery for visiting exhibits.

*Stevenson Student Union Gallery*                         482-6461
*On Siskiyou Blvd. just past Mountain Ave.*
*Open Monday to Friday, 8 AM to 7 PM (6 PM on Fridays)*
New exhibits each month.

*Central Hall Art Gallery*                                 482-6386
*Open 8 AM to Noon, Monday through Thursday in summer,*
*Open to 5 PM and on Fridays during the school year*
Student work for bachelor of fine arts degrees.

*Chappell-Swedenburg House Museum*                        488-1341
*Siskiyou Blvd. at Mountain*
The local headquarters of the Southern Oregon Historical Society
See page 75.

And back near downtown Ashland there is an unusual institution:

*Shakespeare Art Museum*  488-0332
*460 B St., between 3rd and 4th Sts.*
*Open April to October, daily except Tuesdays, 10 AM to 5 PM*

Original art on themes from Shakespeare's plays, gallery talks and seminars, and a museum store, located in an old house in the railroad district.

In nearby cities there are a number of museums worth a visit:

*Jacksonville Doll Museum*  899-7647
*255 E. California, Jacksonville*

Period dolls and doll furnishings.

*Jacksonville Museum*  899-1847
*Children's Museum*
*Southern Oregon Archive*  826-4908

See page 80 for more information about the Southern Oregon Historical Society's museums in Jacksonville.

*Crater Rock Museum*  664-1355
*2002 Scenic Ave., Central Point*
*9 AM to 5 PM daily*

Minerals, petrified wood and semi-precious stones

*Eagle Point Museum*
*North Royal Avenue, Eagle Point*

A small museum of local pioneer history; open Saturdays.

*Butte Creek Mill General Store Museum*  826-3531
*402 Royal Ave., Eagle Point*

A labor of love for the mill owner and not always open, so check first; the Mill itself is listed on the National Register of Historic Places *(see page 84).*

*Grants Pass Museum of Art*  479-3290
*East Park St., in Riverside Park, Grants Pass*
*Noon to 4 PM, Tuesday through Saturday*

Changing exhibits.

*Wiseman Gallery*  479-5541
*Rogue Community College, Grants Pass*
*Monday through Friday, 8 AM to 10 PM (5 PM on Friday)*

Changing exhibits of fine art.

*Old Oregon Historical Museum*                    *855-1043*
*2335 Sardine Creek Rd., Gold Hill*
Indian artifacts, guns, music boxes and antique equipment.

*Favell Museum*                                    *882-9996*
*125 West Main St., Klamath Falls*
*9:30 AM to 5:30 PM, Monday through Saturday*
A huge collection of Indian artifacts, miniature guns and contemporary western art.

*Klamath County Museum*                       *882-2501, ext. 208*
*1451 Main St., Klamath Falls*
*10 AM to 4PM, Tuesday through Saturday*
Local history, anthropology and natural history.

*The Baldwin Hotel Museum*
*31 Main St., Klamath Falls*
*10 AM to 4 PM, Tuesday through Saturday*
A turn-of-the century hotel with original furnishings, it is operated as a branch of the Klamath County Museum.

*Collier State Park Logging Museum*
*On Highway 97 near Chiloquin, 30 miles north of Klamath Falls*
Outdoor display of logging equipment and pioneer cabins.

## OTHER POSSIBILITIES

The Shakespearean Studies Program can also provide special educational programs for independently organized groups. If the group is interested in on-campus housing, it must be educational in nature and meet certain requirements as to class time and instructors. For details for group visitors you should contact:

*Division of Continuing Education*                 *482-6375*
*Conferences Office*
*Southern Oregon State College*

If you have thought of retiring to some scenic place to run an inn, this workshop could be a profitable as well as entertaining way to spend a weekend; several of Ashland's successful B&B's are run by graduates.

*Bed & Breakfast Innkeeping Workshops*             *482-1919*
*Jim and Nancy Beaver*

*Chanticleer Inn*
*120 Gresham St.*

Ashland is also the home of Aletheia, a thirty year old organization devoted to education in various areas related to health and human potential. The director, Jack Schwarz, specializes in biofeedback and pain control. Recent workshops have been devoted to Exploring the Paraconscious, Sexual Energies — The Creative Application of Yin and Yang, and Introduction to Manipulative Therapy, for example, and they give a three day, individualized Personal Health Training as well. For more information or a schedule of upcoming classes contact:

*Aletheia* *488-0701*
*1809 N. Highway 99*

# *Shopping*

Ashland is a great town to wander in, to window shop, and maybe find a treasure or a jolly souvenir. The downtown shopping area is concentrated in six blocks along Main St., between Helman and Third, making it easy to walk around, and the green plaza with the historic buildings facing it is as charming a city scene as you could ask for.

These blocks, with short digressions onto some of the side streets, are perfect for browsing visitors. Many of the stores are open seven days a week in summer, but to guarantee seeing everything, try to go on a weekday other than Monday. As a bonus, the crowds will be much smaller than on weekends.

## TOURIST DELIGHTS

The plaza area is full of stores that are impossible to categorize but well designed to entertain visitors. Two of the stores below Alex's Restaurant, in a restored 1905 building painted pale green, are a good example. They are:

*The Oregon Store*
*39 North Main St.*
Oregon-made jewelry and crafts fill the front of the store, but at the rear there are racks of Oregon wines and a refrigerated meat case with beef jerky and smoked salmon, with samples to taste.

*Iron Buffalo*
*Downstairs, under the Oregon Store*
Leather work of all kinds, from sheepskin slippers to designer clothing.

Don't miss the beaded, fringed, feather decorated, leather bikinis that are often on display in the window.

And next door is the biggest and most diverse of them all:

*Rare Earth*

*37 North Main St.*

This used to be Haight-Ashland; the head shop paraphernalia is gone but the vibes linger. They still have piles of India print bed spreads and baskets for sale, along with Oriental gifts, jewelry, cotton clothes, masks, Body Shop cosmetics, and in the recently developed lower floor, records, tapes, posters and video rentals. Nice things hide among all this merchandise.

Three more places to browse through are on the other side of Main Street:

*Arty Shirts*

*88 North Main St., just north of the plaza*

T-shirts, of course, and lots of other clothes to decorate with transfer designs and messages; you can make personal Shakespeare souvenirs with your favorite quotations.

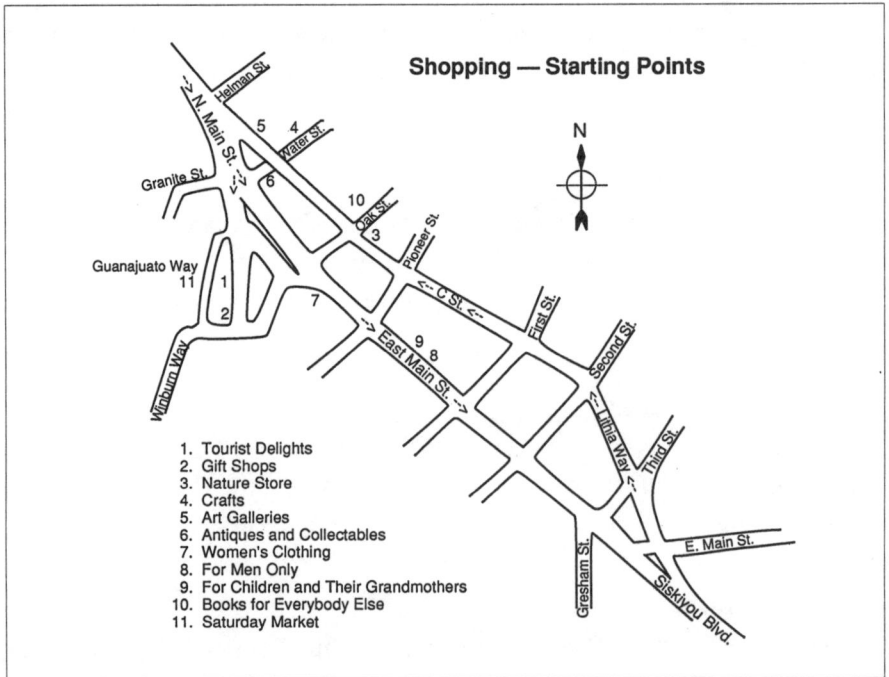

**Shopping — Starting Points**

1. Tourist Delights
2. Gift Shops
3. Nature Store
4. Crafts
5. Art Galleries
6. Antiques and Collectables
7. Women's Clothing
8. For Men Only
9. For Children and Their Grandmothers
10. Books for Everybody Else
11. Saturday Market

*Nimbus*
*25 East Main St., opposite the lower end of the plaza*
Expensive and interesting handcraft items including furniture, ceramics, glass and jewelry take up the first level along with cards and some less expensive ceramics. On two lower levels that step down from there to connect with the Orchard Lane Mall are first men's and then women's clothing.

*Paddington Station*
*125 East Main St., just beyond Pioneer*
A wildly miscellaneous collection of gifts, cards, souvenir shirts, candy and women's clothing and accessories. The English theme comes and goes in the upstairs merchandise and is reasserted downstairs in the (London) Underground Deli.

And perhaps best of all:
*The Tudor Guild Shop*
*15 South Pioneer St., opening off the festival's brick courtyard*
T-shirts, bags and other clothing with Shakespeare quotations; books on Shakespeare and the festival and copies of the plays; English merchandise of all sorts including soaps, marmalade and jam, china cups, place mats; cards, jewelry and miscellany, all with a Shakespearean theme.

## GIFT SHOPS

More of the same on a smaller scale, walking from Lithia Park along the plaza and then south and east along Main St.:
*Myrtlewood Chalet*
*11 North Main, on the plaza near the park*
Traditional wooden gifts from a company established in 1911.

*City Farmhouse*
*30 North Main St., across from the bottom of the plaza*
Stuffed animals, lace curtains and assorted decorative nonsense.

*Paul Bunyan Burlwood Gallery*
*93 Oak St., around the corner off Main St.*
A small shop with some different things; look for the tiny houses carved from weathered wood.

*Titania's Carousel*
*14 South First, across East Main St.*
Another little shop with plush animals and other different gifts.

## NATURE STORE

There is also an unusual shop a block below the plaza, just on the other side of C St. (the street that's one way going north):
*The Northwest Nature Shop*
*154 Oak St.*
Books, prints, crafts, T-shirts and other objects relating to nature and to birds in particular; the owners are recently retired from working with the Audubon Society.

## CRAFTS

Craft shops and galleries are scattered around town; three that are near the Nature Shop are:
*Lithia Creek Arts*
*31 Water St., between North Main and C Streets*
Quality ceramics, jewelry, textiles, glass, and more. Look for the witty stuffed dragons, dinosaurs and four-legged fish.

*Hands-All-Around Quilts*
*150 North Pioneer St., just below C St.*
Everything for quilting enthusiasts, from supplies and fabrics to finished quilts; they give classes and will take orders for quilts, too.

*The von Grabill Collection*
*199 East Main St., at First St.*
Wearable art, jewelry and fine crafts, all hand made in the U.S.

And four more specialized, craft shops, starting north of the plaza:
*The Websters*
*10 Guanajuato Way (the path between the creek and the backs of the plaza stores, named after Ashland's sister city) at Winburn Way*
Hand woven clothing and weaving supplies.

*Family Tree*
*130 East Main St., behind the Stagedoor Cafe's terrace*
A small selection of stained glass

*Ashland Graphics*
*207 Enders Alley, off S. Second St. just above E. Main*
Silk screened T-shirts, calendars, cards and posters

*Amir Kunzler Porcelain Pottery*
*542 A St., across from the tracks in the old railroad district*
Mostly traditional shapes with swirly, multicolored glazes

## ART GALLERIES

Two Galleries are located on North Main between Water and Helman:
*Hanson Howard Gallery*
*82 North Main St.*
Changing exhibits of paintings, prints, sculpture and photographs by Oregon and West Coast artists along with some classy craft work; don't miss the brightly painted wood circus figures that interlock like puzzles.

*Spectrum of Arts Gallery*
*92 North Main St.*
A small stock of original water colors and paintings plus crystals, jewelry, and prints.

Three Galleries dealing in prints are located on East Main St.:
*Accents, the Collector's Gallery*
*33 East Main St.*
They specialize in miniature collectables, too.

*Cascade Wildlife Gallery*
*131 East Main St.*
Wildlife is the subject of most of their prints.

*The Framery*
*270 East Main St.*
A more general stock.

## ANTIQUES AND COLLECTABLES

Starting on the east side of North Main, at Water St., opposite the lower end of the plaza, and walking south there are half a dozen places for people who love browsing through old nonsense instead of new:

*Purple Shutter Antiques*
*60 North Main St., at the rear of the parking lot at the corner*
A tiny cottage with a relatively small stock, attractively displayed.

*La Brocante*
*40 North Main St., in the Orchard Lane Mall*
They also sell Guatemalan textiles and clothing.

*Ashland Antique Emporium*
*90 Pioneer St., at C St., a block below Main St.*
You could lose yourself for days picking through the vast piles of stuff here. Most of it is old-but-not-antique, but that doesn't lessen the pleasure of turning up a duplicate of some trivial object from your childhood, a radio or an orange squeezer. There are large and fantastic things here too that may catch your fancy — how about the upper half of a near-life-size giraffe?

*As You Like It Antiques*
*162 Pioneer St., on the other side of C St.*
A permanent yard sale of yet more interesting old junk, with even more inside; the owner claims to be going out of business, but the quantity of her stock could keep her going forever.

Walking back up to East Main St. and crossing to the other side you will find:

*Manning and Morgan*
*252 East Main St.,*
Back on main street in terms of the merchandise, too, though there are old kitchen things here too, along with more substantial antiques.

*Silk Road Trading Co.*
*296 East Main St., in the same block as Manning and Morgan*
Rugs and eastern antiques, lush and exotic.

Two specialized antique dealers are located in the same block, further on along East Main, and back on the other side:

*Ashland Rare Coin and Jewelry*
*341 East Main St.*

*Century Coin*
*399 East Main St.*
They deal in jewelry too.

For Antique Clothes you have to go back to the plaza area:

*RePete Nostalgic Fashions*
*90 North Main St., in the block just north of the plaza*

Could you use a turn of the century wedding dress for $75?

*Renaissance Rose*
*7 Winburn Way, opposite the entrance to Lithia Park*

Recycled, but not antique

Or to the railroad district:

*Ragpickers*
*285 A St., #5*

Used costumes too

## WOMEN'S CLOTHING

Merchants here must believe that only women shop for clothes while on vacation, men's stores are so rare. But for women, Main Street has lots to offer. In addition to the old clothes stores, many of the general tourist stores discussed above have clothing, not just souvenir sweat shirts, but also casual cotton sportswear (at Rare Earth, for instance) and dressy things (at Paddington Station). And wearable art is featured at several of the crafts stores, The von Grabill Collection and The Websters in particular.

The Hargrove Millinery Shop, located on North Main near Helman circa 1906. *Southern Oregon Historical Society*

Starting on East Main St., just below the festival area, a clockwise walk around the clothing stores will bring you to:

*Red's Threads*
*42 East Main St.*

Clothes manufactured for the store in Indonesia; white and multicolored embroidered openwork and dark, dramatic prints.

*Elizabeth of Course*
*40 North Main St., in the Orchard Lane Mall, across the street*

Flowing cotton gauze, tie died patterns and gypsy styles; though not in large sizes, these clothes are becoming to a wide range of figures.

*Mrs. Quinn's Cottage*
*40 North Main St, also in the Orchard Lane Mall*

Icelandic knits and imported woolens.

Just up the block, after the confusing change of name and numbering:
*Fredrica Lawrence - Fine Clothing*
*37 East Main St.*

Designer clothes at upscale prices.

Continuing up that side of East Main St.:
*The Country Girl*
*149 East Main St.*

Dressier and more mature fashions in spite of the name.

*King's Queen Shop*
*247 East Main St.*

Sizes 12 to 52.

Crossing to the other side you find three for the young and casual:
*Sister Moon*
*268 East Main St.*

*Impressions*
*246 East Main St.*

*Desert Republic*
*242 East Main St.*

Men's things too

And continuing along East Main toward the starting point:
*Lithia Park Shoes*
*232 East Main St.*

They used to be located on Winburn Way, across from the park. Women's shoes are also sold at Fortmiller's and Nimbus.

*Fortmiller's Department Store*
*142 East Main St.*

An old-fashioned, small-town department store that's been going for fifty-two years. Men's as well as girl's and women's clothing and shoes.

## FOR MEN ONLY

In addition to what's available at Nimbus, Desert Republic and Fortmiller's, there are only men's things at:

*Jackson's Men's Store*
*167 East Main St.*

## FOR CHILDREN, AND THEIR GRANDMOTHERS

*Ragamuffin*
*161 East Main St., between Pioneer and First Sts.*
Clothes and more for children.

*Small Change*
*5 North Main St., on the plaza near Lithia Park*
A big selection of children's clothes and incidentals.

*Treehouse Books*
*15 North Main St., just down the block from Small Change*
Books for children and their teachers.

## BOOKS FOR EVERYBODY ELSE

Bookstore browsing, from Oak St., just off Main, going southeast:

*Edna's Book Exchange*
*89 Oak St.*

A little shop crammed with used books; they'll take paperbacks in trade. Theatre books are in the back room.

*Soundpeace - Books, Music, Art*
*199 East Main St., at First St.*
A small and unusual stock including metaphysical books, Sanskrit and Tibetan grammars and dictionaries, and materials on dealing with death.

*Blue Dragon Books*
*283 East Main St., in the next block*
Used, out of print and antiquarian books.

*Bloomsbury Books*
*266 East Main St., across the street*

A large, well stocked, general bookstore with convenient evening and weekend hours. Local history, guide books, general reading...

Close to Bloomsbury there is a comic book store, with another a couple of blocks away in the little mall behind Paddington Station:

*Comic Relief*
*264 East Main St.*

*More Fun*
*116 C St. #3*

And last, two bookstores you'll need to drive to:

*Golden Mean Bookstore*
*1253 Siskiyou Blvd.*

Books on Psychology and parapsychology, Eastern philosophy, metaphysics, health and herbalism, astrology and crystals (and the actual crystals, too); self help and self hypnosis tapes, and new age music tapes.

*SOSC Bookstore*
*On Siskiyou, above the information office*

General books, cards and art supplies in addition to texts

And if you're browsing on a Saturday, don't miss:

## SATURDAY MARKET

On summer Saturdays a crafts market is held all along Guanajuato Way, behind the plaza stores. The selection of craft items is unusually varied, with woodwork and clothing as well as jewelry and ceramics. I was particularly drawn to families of carved wooden pigs, lifelike rather than cute, for $20, and colorful, blown glass humming-bird feeders for $18. There is live music and at least once the Oregon Store served a barbecued salmon lunch for a bargain price.

# *Holidays*

If you come to Ashland on a major holiday you may get in on the fun of a small town celebration. The Ashland Rotary Club sponsors an Easter Egg Hunt in Lithia Park for children up to age 9. There is a giant block party for Halloween preceded by weeks of costume fever in the local stores. And in December there is a Twelve Days of Christmas celebration with craft sales, caroling and theatrical performances.

In Ashland, almost any occasion seems to be a good excuse for a parade. Ashland High School's homecoming brought out the school band, several floats, an endless stream of convertibles with class princesses, the oldest graduate, and the lawn chair drill team whose low precision antics are a entertaining spoof of military drill.

The Fourth of July is the big blowout. The Shakespeare Festival participates in the parade, usually with inspired silliness like the sphinx with Shakespeare's face accompanied by a chorus of peculiar Egyptians that won a prize in 1985. After the parade everybody goes to Lithia Park for a giant crafts fair and an old fashioned program of entertainment and speeches at the band shell. In the evening there are fireworks, of course, set off over the campus but visible all over town. There is also a big celebration of the fourth at Emigrant Lake, with fireworks on a different night, so you can see both if you want.

Some of the bed and breakfast inns and restaurants stage holiday activities, particularly in the slow season, when they need to generate business. Chata presents a traditional Polish Christmas Eve dinner and a soup buffet on New Year's Day. The Winchester Inn offers several

Fourth of July, 1912. *Ashland Public Library, print by Terry Skibby*

harvest festival dinners in November and Dickens Feasts in December as well as serving a special menu on Thanksgiving. The Ashland Hills Inn also presents Dickens Feasts, with entertainment, and serves buffet dinners on Thanksgiving and Christmas. They stage a New Year's Eve party with music and dancing and offer a package that includes accommodations and brunch.

The Winchester Inn, Cowslip's Belle Lodging and Highland Acres have all staged Murder Mystery Weekends, a sort of do-it-yourself theatre for when the festival isn't providing any. Guests are given some advance information as to their assigned characters so they can be prepared to drop clues as necessary to advance the plot, but the solution is up to the players.

Several nearby towns have local festivities that might fit in with your vacation plans. Medford's early April Pear Blossom Festival includes a parade, a street fair and a band contest. Rogue River has a Rooster Crowing Contest on the last Saturday in June. Gold Hill celebrates the old west with Gold Dust Days in July. In August, the Prospect Jamboree lets you watch loggers at work. And of course, there's a county fair that's held in Central Point in July. About the best source of dates and details is the Southern Oregon Recreation Supplement that the local papers distribute in late spring. Or for advance information, you could try:

*Medford Chamber of Commerce*          772-6293
*304 S. Central Ave., Medford*

Bright lights and Christmas decorations on Main Street from just north of the plaza. *Ashland Chamber of Commerce, Medford Mail Tribune*

71

"Firehouse Five" in Ashland's Old Fashioned 4th of July Parade. *Ashland Visitor's Bureau, photo by Kevin Carpenter*

# *Touring*

## EXPLORING ASHLAND

This is a town planned before there were cars and well scaled for people to walk in. If you get out of your car you see the quirky little things that accumulate in an old place and give it character. My pet discoveries include:

• The plaque on the huge cypress at the corner of Laurel and North Main that commemorates its planting in 1905;

• The modern, shingled building further down Laurel, between Van Ness and Hersey Streets, with the shingled thunderbird on its wall, two storeys high;

• The fantasy fence at 337 Oak Street, all curves and very sixties;

•The iris fancier's garden at the corner of Third and B Streets which I can't wait to catch in full bloom.

If you walk, you're bound to find things you will treasure, the more so because you discovered them yourself.

Lithia Park is the place for cool walks on hot days. A booklet that's available from the park office identifies nearly a hundred trees on a self-guiding trail. The trail is only a mile long, but finding the markers and reading the text makes it take about two hours to complete. If you want to feed the ducks, food is for sale at the Creek View Cafe, just across from the park on Winburn Way.

The braille trail and par course seem to have fallen into disrepair, but the local AARP and the Community Hospital have recently sponsored the installation of a six station, 1.5 mile walkersize course with recommended times and exercises for strengthening the heart and other muscles. It starts across the creek from the upper duck pond; there's a path from the parking area just beyond the pond to a bridge over the creek.

And there are lots of paths, both paved and wild, to wander on. If you come from a city where parks are no longer considered safe for solitary walks you will be reassured by the constant presence of park workers and police here. I commented to one young policeman about a fierce dog I had seen in a jeep I had parked near; he had already observed the dog and knew just which car was mine.

There is also a network of unpaved roads starting at the top of Lithia Park that are favored by joggers and people out for a quiet walk. The roads wind around in the hills above town and connect to the city streets at various points. Interesting new houses are being built on these hill roads as the city expands.

The Ashland Loop Road, which starts at the end of Terrace St., is many miles of slow, dusty meandering through the woods if you choose to drive all of it, but about two and a half miles along the left fork there is a parking area and a half-mile self-guiding nature trail. The Oredson-Todd Woods Trail is another half mile walk; it begins near Green Meadows Way, which crosses Tolman Creek Road at the southern end of Ashland.

## ASHLAND'S PAST

If you're intrigued by local pioneer history or old buildings you have come to the right place. Ashland and the surrounding country are rich in pioneer relics, more having survived here than in places that have prospered more and grown faster. That's not to say that nothing of value has been lost. Fires, the realignment of East Main St. and commercial development have all removed old buildings that we would enjoy having in Ashland today. Only twenty five years ago the site of the incongruously modern First Interstate Bank on East Main was occupied by a big hotel, a turreted Victorian remodeled in mission style, that wouldn't be demolished today without a fight. (Photographs on pages 118 and 121.)

To learn more about vanished Ashland as well as what remains to be enjoyed today, the Southern Oregon Historical Society's museum is the place to start. It's a grand old house that has been totally renovated and now contains changing exhibits on Ashland history. There are also collections of genealogical material and historical photographs available for research. Don't miss the samples from the layers of wallpaper removed during the renovation; the series of nine from the kitchen are a mini history of domestic decor.

The Historical Society takes groups on guided walks of the plaza area, going into the residential area above North Main Street where many of the early settlers' houses are, and of the railroad district. The guide brings along old photographs from the society's collection and shares anecdotes about the early residents. One Sunday each year they put on an old fashioned Lawn Social, serving strawberries and ice cream while musicians play on the front porch. If you want to spend an afternoon in antique style, or take one of the guided walks, call the museum for the schedule:

*Chappell Swedenburg House*        *488-1341*
*990 Siskiyou Blvd., at Mountain Ave.*
*Open Tuesday to Saturday, 1 PM to 5 PM*

The old Ashland Cemetery on East Main is full of interesting monuments. Anne Hill Russell, one of the first white women to come to Ashland, married a marble cutter and learned the business herself. The story is that she also founded the local branch of the Women's Christian Temperance Union and carved its symbol, a white bow, on her gravestones. If you like poking around old graveyards, this one should be good for a shady afternoon ramble. The Mountain View Cemetery, at Ashland and Normal Sts., is the site of an Egyptian Style mausoleum built in 1924 that's also worth a visit by monument lovers.

Twenty-nine Ashland buildings and Lithia Park are listed on the National Register of Historic Places. If you enjoy walking, you'll see many fine examples of late nineteenth and early twentieth century architecture in Ashland's older neighborhoods. Except near the Southern Oregon State campus, where few old buildings have survived the college's expansion, the listed buildings have interesting neighbors, equally old in many cases though not on the register. The places are listed roughly north to south, but a map will help you find some of the back streets.

If you want more information on these and many other historic buildings in Ashland, Medford and the surrounding countryside, the SOSC library has a copy of an annotated list compiled by Kay Atwood and

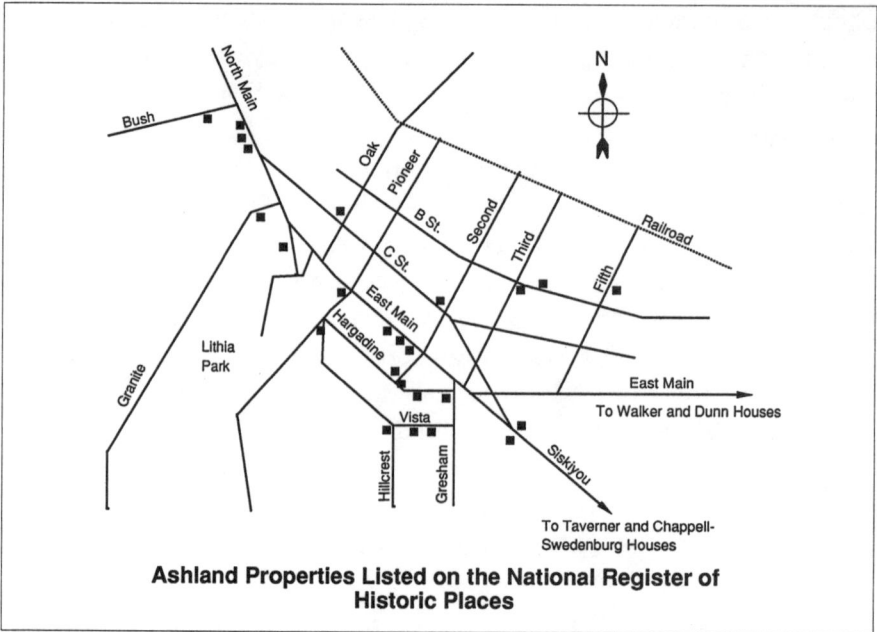

**Ashland Properties Listed on the National Register of Historic Places**

L. Scott Clay for a tour by the Northern Pacific Coast Chapter of the Society of Architectural Historians in 1981. For more detail on the buildings in the plaza/North Main area, there is a leaflet titled "Self Guided Walking Tour of Historic Sites and Buildings in the Oldest Part of Ashland, Oregon" that the Chamber of Commerce distributes for the Ashland Heritage Committee. It is illustrated with pictures of buildings that are gone now so you can see what used to be where you are walking.

There are six National Register properties in the North Main/plaza area (the Heritage Committee leaflet points out twenty more that are worth noting though they're not on the National Register.):

*Richard Posey Campbell House (1888)*
*94 Bush St.*

Constructed by Orlando Coolidge as a rental and initially occupied by his daughter's family.

*Orlando Coolidge House (1875 )*
*137 North Main St.*

The first of the grand Victorians known as the Three Sisters; Coolidge was a pioneer nurseryman.

*Isaac Woolen House (1876-1881)*
*131 North Main St.*
Another Sister, it was enlarged and moved to line up with its neighbors in 1881.

*W.H. Atkinson House (1880)*
*125 North Main St.*
The third Sister, now the Queen Anne B&B.

*Domingo Perozzi House (1902)*
*88 Granite St.*
Perozzi operated a dairy located about where the Creek View Cafe is today, a short walk away on Winburn Way.

*IOOF Building (1879-1880)*
*49-57 North Main St.*
One of several buildings facing the plaza that were built in brick after a fire in 1879. The Heritage Committee leaflet identifies others on this block, including some now gone.

In the downtown area :

*J.M. McCall House (1883)*
*153 Oak St.*
Now a B&B; McCall owned the woolen mill that was a major industry before it burned in another spectacular fire.

*First National Bank, Vaupel Store and Oregon Hotel (1909-1910)*
*15 South Pioneer St.*
Now occupied by the Festival Exhibit Center

*Lithia Springs Hotel (1924-1925)*
*212 East Main St.*
Now called the Mark Antony; the elevator tower on the north side was added when the hotel was reopened, though no elevator has been installed.

*Citizens Banking and Trust Company Building (1910)*
*232-242 East Main St.*

*The Enders Building (1910-1914)*
*250-300 East Main St.*
Designed by local architect Frank C. Clark who also designed the Library and the Chappell-Swedenburg house. The Columbian Hotel is upstairs.

*Fordyce Roper House/Southern Oregon Hospital (1886)*
*35 South Second St.*

Originally located on Main St., it has been moved, partially burned and now, much remodeled inside, it is the Winchester Inn. (Photograph on page 147)

*First Baptist Church (1911)*
*241 Hargadine St.*

The "old pink church" that is now the Oregon Cabaret Theatre.

*Baldwin Beach House (1884)*
*348 Hargadine St.*

*E.V. Carter House (1886)*
*505 Siskiyou Blvd.*

Moved from across the street when the Carters built number 514.

*Carter-Fortmiller House (1909)*
*514 Siskiyou Blvd.*

Now the RoyAl Carter House B&B.

And higher on the hill above Main Street there are:

*Amos & Vera Nininger House (1909-1910)*
*80 Hargadine St.*

The Stone House (lodgings for visitors), across from the Elizabethan Theater in the triangle between Pioneer and Fork Streets, at Hargadine.

*Humboldt Pracht House (1910)*
*234 Vista St.*

A bungalow designed by the leading local architect, Frank C. Clark

*Eddings-Provost House (1889)*
*364 Vista St.*

*Boslough-Claycomb (1913)*
*1 Hillcrest*

*H.B. Carter House (1888)*
*91 Gresham St.*

The Carters were the original bankers in town.

On the other side of Main Street, in the district where the railroad workers lived, there are more modest structures that have survived because there was a period of depression after the railroad jobs were lost. When better times came, the city expanded into other areas.

*Trinity Episcopal Church (1894-1895)*
*44 North Second St.*

*Colonel William H. Silsby House (1896)*
*111 Third St.*

*E.C. Kane House (1886)*
*386 B St.*

*Nils Ahlstrom House (1888)*
*248 Fifth St.*

Ahlstrom worked for the railroad.

Further out Siskiyou, near the SOSC Campus are two designs by local architect, Frank Clark:

*George Taverner House (1904)*
*912 Siskiyou Blvd.*

*The Chappell-Swedenburg House (1904-1905)*
*990 Siskiyou Blvd.*

The Southern Oregon Historical Society Museum

On the outskirts of town are two of the earliest surviving structures:

*John P. Walker House (1856-1858)*
*1521 East Main St.*

*Patrick Dunn Ranch (1860)*
*4224 Hwy. 66*

Dunn was one of the earliest settlers; he later moved to a house at 65 Granite St. that is still occupied by members of his family.

## JACKSONVILLE

The Jacksonville Historic District is only a few miles from Ashland, but it's about a hundred years back in time. Declining gold mining and the rerouting of the railroad, and finally the relocation of the county seat to Medford, helped freeze Jacksonville somewhere in the last century. You can get there by going west from Medford, on Highway 238. From Ashland, you can take route 99N and South Stage Road, which is the prettier route.

Downtown Jacksonville is listed on the National Register of Historic Places in its entirety. The U.S. Bank distributes a folder with an admirably clear map and descriptions of eighty-six historic buildings and other points of interest. It is available at the Jacksonville Museum as well as from the bank. You can easily use it for a self-guided walking tour of as much of the town as you like, or you can take one of the guided walks conducted by the Southern Oregon Historical Society in the summer months. Also in summer there are (motorized) trolley tours leaving hourly from the Beekman Bank building at Third and California Streets.

The Southern Oregon Historical Society is headquartered in Jacksonville, where they operate three museums, three historic buildings, a research library and a historical archive.

The Jacksonville Museum is located in the old courthouse that was abandoned when the railroad was rerouted and the county seat moved to Medford, in 1926. The museum displays include Peter Britt's photographic equipment and some spectacular clothes, among them three Paris dresses from 1910-20 that suggest Southern

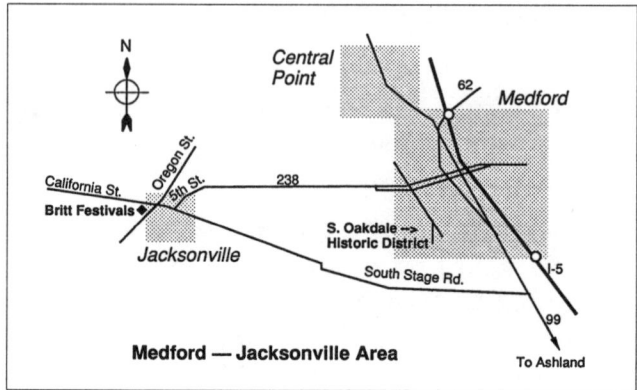

Medford — Jacksonville Area

Oregon had come a long way since the pioneers fought the Indians sixty years earlier. There is a reference library and an extensive collection of historic photographs with cooperative staff to assist anyone who wants to use them. SOHS also operates a museum about and for children in a building next door to the court house.

*Southern Oregon Historical Society*          *899-1847*
*Jacksonville Museum and Children's Museum*
*206 North Fifth St.*
*Open daily 10 AM to 5 PM, closed Mondays, Labor Day to Memorial Day*

During the summer months the Historical Society staffs several historic buildings so they can be toured. These include the Beekman House and Bank. There are also museum exhibits visible through the Third Street windows of the U.S. Hotel. The Society operates the

Southern Oregon Archive in cooperation with Jackson County, too. It contains county records from the 1850's on, plus other documents and books, all available to the public for research.

*Southern Oregon Archive*                      *826-4908*
*320 Antelope Rd., off Oregon route 62*
*Open Monday to Friday, 1 PM to 5 PM*

Jacksonville is the home of the Peter Britt Festivals. When there are no performances scheduled the festival grounds are open to the public to explore; it's a county park, located just south of California St., above First. There's a view over the valley and a nice breeze here; the tables under the trees are a pleasant place to picnic.

Heading north from Britt Park along Oregon St. you will find the old cemetery; it's up a winding drive to the left, at E St., and is worth exploring. A little farther out on Oregon is the Catalog House, a huge and exuberant Queen Anne that was reputedly ordered out of a catalog and shipped in eleven boxcars. Officially it's the Nunan House and is number 51 in the U.S. Bank's leaflet.

If you decide you want to stay in Jacksonville, accommodations are described starting on page 155, restaurants beginning on page 185, and the Tasting Room, an unusual source of picnic food, on page 83.

For more information about Jacksonville, contact the Chamber of Commerce; in summer they operate an office in the old depot, at Oregon and C Streets:

*Jacksonville Chamber of Commerce*              *899-8118*
*185 North Oregon St.*

If you want to ramble around more historic areas in Jackson County, The Historical Society distributes a leaflet called "Historic Jackson County" in which twenty three points of interest are described. A fact sheet on each of them is available from the Society. SOHS is also the publisher of a book by Marjorie O'Harra called *Southern Oregon: Short Trips Into History* . She combines historical anecdotes with maps and directions for finding the places she writes about.

## Medford

Medford tends to be shunted aside with the same sort of disdain that inspired Gertrude Stein's remark about Oakland, that "there is no there, there." Visitors tend to think of it as an airport and a shopping center, and after learning a little local history, as the place that supplanted Ashland as the railroad center, and Jacksonville as the county seat.

But Medford is only a little younger than Ashland and Jacksonville. Twenty places in Medford are listed in the National Register, including the art deco Jackson County Courthouse, the Carnegie Library, and the South Oakdale Historic District. South Oakdale Avenue crosses Highway 238, the road to Jacksonville out of Medford, a few blocks west of the freeway (I-5) and there are historic buildings on neighboring streets that make the area worth exploring.

Of course, Medford has a history of its own, and the buildings in the South Oakdale area are not only architecturally interesting, they are also the homes of some of the leading characters in Medford's dramatic past. According to Atwood and Clay's notes for the architectural historians, two county judges lived a block apart at numbers 408 and 504 South Oakdale in the 1930's. They were on opposite sides of a controversial scheme called the Good Government Congress that was intended to take control of local government. The one who lived at number 504 went to jail.

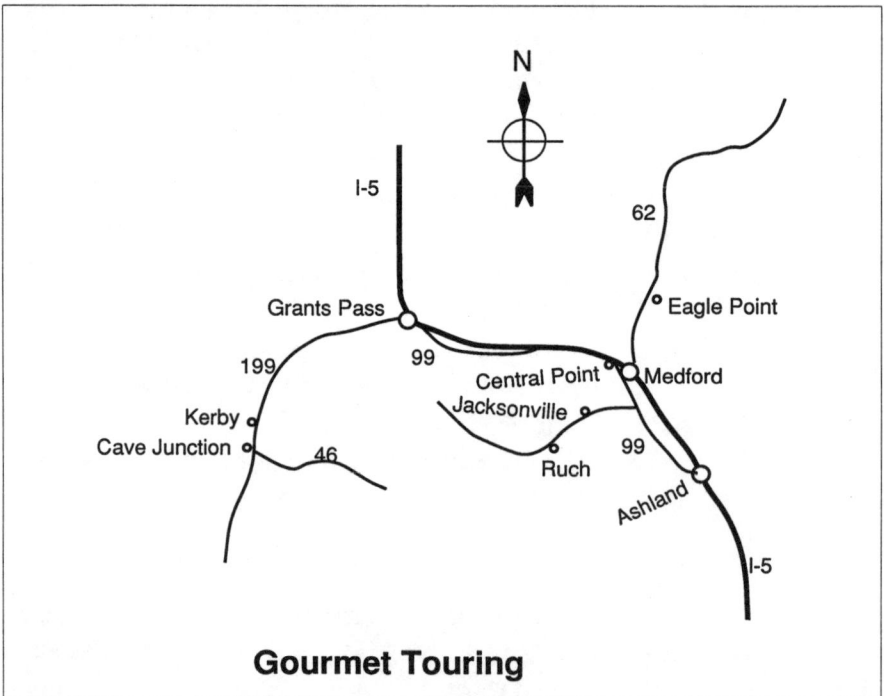

**Gourmet Touring**

If this intrigues you, you can investigate further through the Southern Oregon Historical Society (see above) or possibly at the Medford Library:

*Jackson County Library System*                              *776-7281*
*413 W. Main St., Medford*

## GOURMET TOURING

Oregon foods and wines are available to taste and buy in Ashland and at a number of other places nearby. If food and wine are your thing, you might enjoy some of the following places. Starting in Ashland:

*Valley View Tasting Room*
*52 East Main St.*

The products of the one vineyard are quite varied and the sales people are very free with the samples. If you find you enjoy Oregon wines, you can order them in most of the restaurants in the Ashland area.

*The Oregon Store*
*39 North Main St.*

Several kinds of beef jerky and smoked salmon can be tasted and bought at the rear of the store; they sell Oregon wines, too.

*Pyramid Juice Company*                                  *482-2292*
*160 Helman St.*

They have taken fruit juice way beyond apple and grape; watermelon is a lovely refreshing taste as well as a beautiful color, and they make many other unusual juices and blends. Tasting hours are limited, so call first. Continuing north, out of Ashland:

*Harry and David's*                                        *776-2277*
*2836 S. Pacific Highway (99N)*

They sell produce, including the famous pears in the late fall, Jackson Perkins roses, Oregon specialty foods and wines, gift items and deli sandwiches. There is a restaurant (see page 207) and you can tour the plant where they pack the gift baskets. To avoid waiting, call in advance for tour reservations.

*The Tasting Room*                                        *899-1829*
*690 N. Fifth St., Jacksonville*
On Highway 238 east of Jacksonville
This is a tasting room for Valley View wines, Pinnacle Orchards fruit

and specialty foods, and Gary R. West sausages and smoked meats. They make deli sandwiches with the meats, and you can buy fruit and wine to complete a tasty picnic. Some unusually attractive country style gifts are for sale here, too.

*Rogue River Vineyards*
*230 East C St.*

A small tasting room for a different vineyard's wines, located across from the Jacksonville Museum.

*Valley View Vineyard* 899-5468
*1000 Applegate Rd., Ruch, 8 miles west of Jacksonville on route 238*

Informal tours and tasting available every day.

*Rogue River Valley Creamery* 664-2233
*311 N. Front St.*
*Central Point, north of Jacksonville and Medford, on route 99*

There is a sales room here — they sell all kinds of cheese though they make only cheddar, jack and blue.— and a viewing window into the plant. The best time to see them making cheese is between ten and eleven on Monday mornings.

*Butte Creek Mill* 826-3531
*In Eagle Point, 10 miles north of Medford on route 62*
*Monday to Saturday, 9 AM to 5 PM*

An 1872 water powered grist mill, listed on the National Register of Historic Places and really ancient looking still; they sell stone ground flour plus other natural grain products, nuts and dried fruits, at the mill and by mail. The owner's hobby is a museum in which he has recreated an old general store. It's in a separate building and isn't always open, so if you want to see it as well as the mill, call first.

Most of southern Oregon's wineries are farther north, in the Roseburg area, but in addition to Valley View, there are wineries to visit to the west of Ashland, near Grants Pass and Cave Junction:

*Bridgeview Vineyards* 592-4688
*4210 Holland Loop Rd.*
*Cave Junction*

Tours by appointment only; tasting room on Hwy. 199 in Kerby, across from the Kerbyville Museum, open daily from May through October, 11 AM to 5 PM.

> *Rogue River Vineyards*                                    *476-1051*
> *3145 Helms Rd., Grants Pass, off the road to Cave Junction*

Tours and tasting, of both varietal and fruit flavored wines.

> *Siskiyou Vineyard*                                    *592-3727*
> *6220 Caves Highway, 6 miles east of Cave Junction on Hwy. 46*

Tasting and sales room open daily 11 AM to 4 PM; they also have a nature trail and picnic area at the winery and sponsor a spring wine festival.

If you are interested in more information on Oregon wines a directory with maps and descriptions of vineyards is available from:

> *Oregon Winegrowers Association*                                    *233-2377*
> *P.O. Box 6590*
> *Portland, OR 97228*

You might also enjoy Ashland's newly organized winter wine and food festival, A Taste of Ashland. Tastings, special dinners, educational

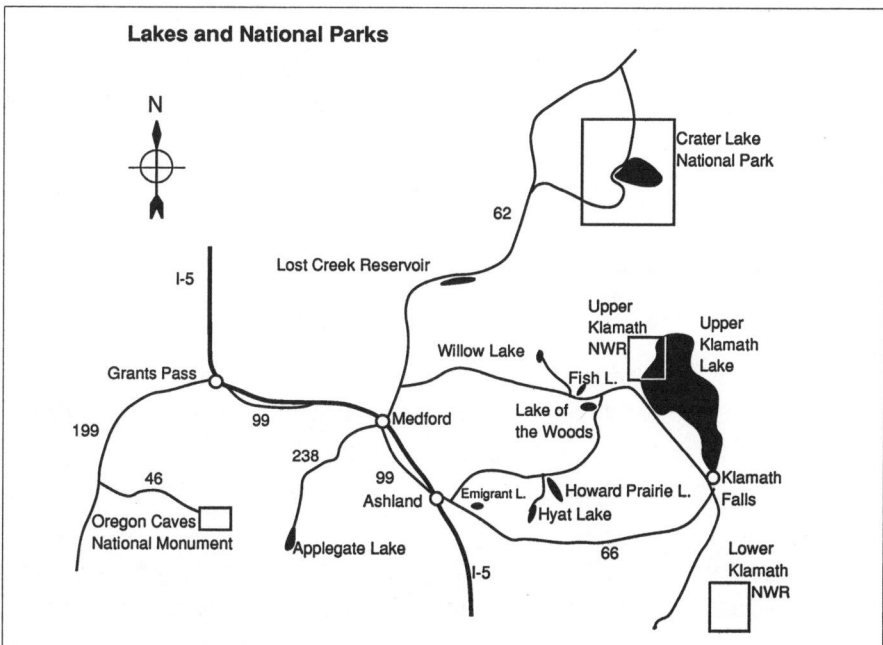

Lakes and National Parks

programs and a cooking competition were scheduled for February, 1988. For the exact dates and a list of the current year's events, contact:

*Ashland Chamber of Commerce*          482-3486

## A Day by a Lake

Lakes, lots of lakes — except in times of drought they are all good for swimming, boating, sailing and fishing. There are resorts, county parks, camp grounds, food services and boating facilities in varying assortments on all of them. The resort telephone numbers are included in each listing; for information about the Jackson County Parks, contact:

*Parks and Recreation Department*          776-7001
*Jackson County Courthouse*
*Medford, OR 97501*

Ask for their leaflet, "Outdoor Opportunities: Jackson County Parks."

Going generally east from Ashland there are:

*Emigrant Lake*          488-0595 *(marina)*
*5 miles from Ashland on Hwy. 66*

This is a small reservoir created in a rather flat, treeless valley. Even though many trees have been planted and there's scrub oak, too, it looks hot and dry. There are areas for picnicking and camping, a giant water slide, and a concession stand as well as a marina with boat rentals and instruction. In a dry year, Emigrant Lake can be reduced to a mud puddle, leaving a band of bare ground between the water and the facilities.

*Hyatt Lake*          482-0525
*Off Dead Indian Rd.*

This is another shallow lake in a flat valley. There are evergreen trees, but a lot of ugly mud flats show when the water is low. There is a park and a resort with cabins, camping, boating facilities, and a restaurant. There's also a Winter Play Area off Hyatt Prairie Road, with cross country skiing and sled runs, ice skating and skate rentals.

*Howard Prairie Lake*          482-1979
*About 22 Miles along Dead Indian Road*

This one looks like a lake should, even in the fall of a dry year. There are several parks with camping, picnicking and boating facilities and a resort with a store, a restaurant and boat and fishing tackle rental. Sailboat races take place here in June and a triathlon in August. Watch for the old log Lilyglen Barn at the north end of the lake, on Dead Indian Road; it's the last remaining building from an early ranch, but it's still in usable condition.

> *Lake of the Woods*                                              949-8300
> *At Dead Indian Rd. and Highway 140*
>
> *Fish Lake*                                                       949-8500
> *A short distance west on Highway 140*

Lake of the Woods looks handsome and is heavily developed with summer houses. There is a resort, with a lodge, cabins, camping and RV hookups, boat and tackle rental, store and restaurant; there is also cross country skiing, ice fishing, skating, and snowmobiling here in winter, with ski and skate rentals available. There are similar facilities at the nearby but smaller Fish Lake Resort.

> *Willow Lake*                                                     865-3229
> *Off Highway 140, west of Mt. McLoughlin*

The resort at Willow Lake is farther off the main road, near the town of Butte Falls. It offers the usual cabins and campsites and boating facilities, and there is a restaurant.

> *Upper Klamath Lake*
> *On Highway 140 beyond Lake of the Woods*

This is the largest lake in Oregon, with resorts and the National Wildlife Refuge (see below) on the northwest side and more tourist facilities at the southern end, near Klamath Falls.

West of Ashland, you will find:

> *Applegate Lake*
> *Off Highway 238 out of Ruch,*

This is a flood control project, and is also used to insure adequate summer flows and cool enough temperatures for the salmon and steelhead to flourish in the Applegate and Rogue Rivers. The Forest Service operates hike-in campgrounds with minimal facilities and there are day use areas for swimming and picnicking and a boat launching ramp, but most of the shoreline has been kept in a natural state. For more information contact:

*U.S Forest Service*                                                   *899-1812*
*Rogue River National Forest*
*Star Ranger Station*
*6941 Upper Applegate Rd., Jacksonville*

Going North out of Medford you'll find:
*Lost Creek Reservoir*                                      *878-2235*
*About 33 miles past Medford on Highway 62*

There is a picnic area and the fish hatchery (see page 105) at the dam. Joseph P. Stewart State Park has campgrounds, picnic areas and boating facilities, including a marina, docks and launching ramp, and handicapped accessible restrooms.

## NATIONAL PARKS, MONUMENTS AND WILDLIFE REFUGES

Crater Lake National Park is about ninety miles north of Ashland, via route 62 out of Medford. During the summer rooms are available in an antique, shingled hotel, and there are also campgrounds, but if you don't want to spend that much time, it makes a pleasant one-day trip.

To see the lake in summer, there is a 33 mile loop road around the rim that now can be driven in either direction, or for a better view of the crystal clarity of the water, a two hour launch trip around the shoreline. The launches leave from a point about a mile from the road; they cannot operate until the snow on the trail has melted.

Park Service interpretive programs, including a film and exhibits, explain the formation of the lake and there are talks and walks with rangers, too. Food service is available year round and cross country skis can be rented between Thanksgiving and early April. In winter there are also snowshoe walks with the rangers.

*Crater Lake National Park*                             *594-2211*
*Crater Lake, OR 97604*

*Crater Lake Lodge*                                         *594-2511*
*P.O. Box 128, Crater Lake, OR 97604*

Oregon Caves National Monument is about ninety miles west of Ashland via route 199 out of Grants Pass to Cave Junction, where route 46 turns off to the Monument. Every day of the year except Thanksgiving and Christmas, National Park service interpreters lead groups of no more than sixteen visitors on one and a half hour tours of these spectacular caverns . The temperature inside averages 41 degrees and there are 550 steps, so a warm jacket and walking shoes are essential. Also, children under six are not allowed to go, though there is a child care service.

Food and lodging are available in the summer months only. The rustic old Oregon Caves Chateau is an attraction in itself. Built in 1934, it climbs up six levels against the side of the mountain and has a creek running through the dining room. Simple rooms, many with attractive views, cost $50 for two. There are also unimproved campgrounds nearby in the National Forest.

In addition to tours of the caves, the National Monument offers a number of short trails for hikers, including a three quarter mile nature trail with signs identifying the plant life.

*Oregon Caves National Monument*          *592-2100*
*Cave Junction, OR 97523*

*Oregon Caves Chateau*          *592-3400*
*P.O. Box 128, Cave Junction, OR 97523*

The Klamath Basin National Wildlife Refuges are scattered on both sides of the California/Oregon border. A majority of the waterfowl migrating along the Pacific Flyway stop at these refuges, creating peak fall concentrations of nearly a million birds. More than five hundred bald eagles winter here, too. There are no accommodations within the refuges, but visitors can observe and take photographs from self-guided car and canoe routes. Fishing and hunting are also permitted, subject to both state and refuge regulations. For more information, including descriptive leaflets for the canoe trails and regulations for hunters and anglers, contact:

*Refuge Manager*          *916-667-2231*
*U.S. Fish and Wildlife Service*
*Route 1, Box 74*
*Tulelake, CA 96134*

To rent canoes to take on the Upper Klamath Lake trail, call:

*Rocky Point Resort*          *356-2287*

## CLASSIC SUNDAY DRIVES

If you head east on Highway 66 past Emigrant Lake you will have a pleasant drive through scrubby foothills and into densely forested country. The Patrick Dunn Ranch is on your right, as you cross Neil Creek, and the Hill/Dunn cemetery is further along, past the turn-off to the lake. About eighteen miles further you'll come to Tubb Springs Wayside, a state park where traces of the Applegate Trail, which was used by the earliest settlers, can be seen. A few miles more brings you to Lincoln, a lumber company town that is now the Oregon Extension of Houghton College, where honors students get away from New York. If you've developed an appetite, look up the Greensprings Inn on page 206. From there it's about forty five miles to Klamath Falls if you want to continue on. The view as you come back down into the valley is particularly handsome at sunset and after, with the lights coming on in the towns.

Heading north out of Medford on Highway 62 eventually gets you to Crater Lake, but there's lots of pretty country along the way. Just out of Medford is Camp White. Built at the beginning of World War II and now used by the Veteran's Administration as a home for over a thousand disabled veterans, it looks so exactly like an army base should that it feels like a movie set. The Butte Creek Mill is in Eagle Point and there are museums there too (see page 84). At Lost Creek Lake there's the Cole Rivers Hatchery (see page 105) and Joseph Stewart State Park with a

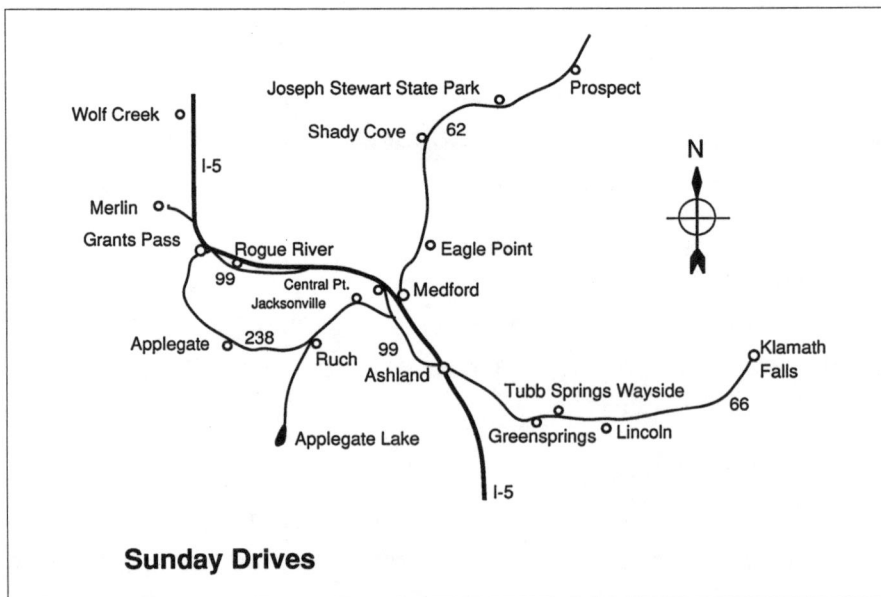

**Sunday Drives**

swimming beach and a marina. And just before you get to Prospect, there's a noted area for river scenery with some of the area's tallest waterfalls (nearly 200 feet); it's reached by taking Mill Creek Drive. If you're driving back at dinner time, consider that Bel Di's in Shady Cove is on your way (see page 204).

Going west from Medford toward Grants Pass you have two choices. The freeway (I-5) gives you sweeping views of the countryside that are not to be seen from old route 99, the Rogue River Highway. On Highway 99 every inch seems to be developed, but there are breaks where you can stop to enjoy the river. The Creamery in Central Point is along the route here (see page 84) as is Valley of the Rogue State Park. On Highway 99, just south of the turn-off for the town of Rogue River, and on your right if you're headed south, is the perfect pioneer home, neither modernized nor in ruins. It's the log house built by David Birdseye in 1855 and still occupied by members of his family, and though you can only look at it from the road, it's not to be missed. At Grant's Pass Highway 99 ends, the freeway turns north and the country becomes less scenic. The Wolf Creek Tavern (see page 210) is about twenty miles further, or if it's already supper time, there is Paradise Ranch (page 209) nearby. If you meandered up the old road, you can speed back on I-5.

If you take Highway 99 north out of Ashland and turn off towards Jacksonville you will go through some of the loveliest farm country in the area. It's suburban into Jacksonville, but on Highway 238 heading toward Ruch you can see flocks of grazing geese and white Arabian horses in the fields. Besides all the attractions of Jacksonville, there is the Logtown cemetery to see, about six miles out of town. A rose that blooms there starting toward the end of May is a cutting from one that a pioneer woman brought from Missouri. Valley View Vineyards is a couple of miles further on, and best visited in the fall when the grapes are being processed. If you take Upper Applegate Rd. out of Ruch you will come to the covered McKee bridge, built in 1917 and listed on the National Register, and then to Flumet Flat Campground where there is a trail through the remains of a hydraulic mining operation; you'll end up at Applegate Lake. Or you can continue on Hwy. 238 to Applegate, where there's Applegate River House if you want to stop (see page 203), and on to Grants Pass.

Australian black swan in upper Lithia Park. Two black swans were presented to the Festival by Traci and Christy Smith in honor of the opening of the Festival's new theatre space, The Black Swan. The Festival in turn presented the swans to the park. In their honor the upper Lithia Park pond is now named "Black Swan Lake" in honor of the birds. *Oregon Shakespearean Festival*

# Outdoor Activities

The Rogue and some of the other rivers in southern Oregon are a major focus of summer recreation. If you want to do something more active than just looking at the water from the road or more organized than swimming in it, a trip with one or another of the river sports companies listed might suit your pleasure. Trips of widely varying character are offered, from relatively sedate sightseeing to whitewater adventures.

You should be aware that there is some risk involved in any river activity and should discuss the age, physical condition and level of experience of the members of your party with the company you choose before selecting a trip. I may be excessively cautious, but I would start with something tame and work up to the longer and more rugged trips, but I have to confess I've never tried any of them. I've listed the companies as a convenience for readers, without recommendation.

There are many other ways to be active and outdoors here besides river trips. I've tried to provide information for the vacation standards — golf, tennis, swimming, riding — and some unusual possibilities as well. If I've never floated down the Rogue, you needn't ask if I've tried parachuting!

The cost for participating in these various activities ranges from absolutely nothing for hiking or playing tennis on the courts in Ashland's parks to the very substantial fees charged for long horseback or river rafting trips. The telephone numbers are included to make it convenient for you to get more information about the things that interest you.

If you're as green as I am about outdoor activities, you might find Ashland's one-stop-shopping and advice service helpful:

*Four Seasons Adventures*                         *482-8352, 488-0583*
*290 Helman St., Ashland*

*Southern Oregon/Ashland Adventure Center*
*31 North Main St. (downstairs at Ashland Mountain Supply)*

They lead river trips, but they also act as agents for other tour leaders; an Adventure Shop in the Rogue Valley Mall where tour packages would be sold is planned for 1988. Bill Hunt, the owner, seemed to me to be willing to find the right trip for me and possibly had more variety to offer than the individual guides and river touring companies which tend to specialize. Four Seasons is involved in a wide variety of sports — cross country and snowboarding as well as downhill skiing, bicycling, fishing, hiking and climbing, among others. They also offer classes and programs in such subjects as backpacking, kayaking, gold mining and wilderness survival. And they rent and sell equipment.

But if you know what you want, just not where to find it, here are the possibilities, from riding in Big Al's hot air balloon to playing in a tennis tournament sponsored by him. In between are listed a variety of other activities that Big Al is not involved in, as far as I know, including upwards of thirty river touring companies besides Four Seasons.

## BALLOON FLIGHTS

*Big Al's Hot Air Balloon Flights*                         *482-3410*
*474 North Main St.*

## BICYCLING

For information on rentals and service, see page 224.

There are bike lanes on a few of the downtown streets in Ashland and a couple of paved bike paths in Medford, the three mile Bear Creek Bike and Nature Trail and the Don Stathos Bikeway which runs four miles along Highway 238, from Columbus Avenue to Jacksonville. For information on the Medford bike trails, call:

*Medford Park Department*                         *770-4586.*

Bike races are announced in the Chamber of Commerce calendar leaflet and in the Ashland Park Department flyer.

## BOWLING

*Rondo Lanes*                                                    *482-1727*
*1505 Siskiyou Blvd.*

## FITNESS, AEROBICS, DANCE AND YOGA

*Ashland Health and Fitness*                                    *482-5510*
*1666 Ashland St., in the Ashland Center*
Aerobics, Nautilus and Universal weights, exercise bikes

*Ashland Stars Gymnastic Academy*                               *482-8800*
*75 B St., at Pioneer St.*

*The Ballet Academy*                                            *482-4789*
The State Ballet of Oregon's school; classes for children and adults.

*Plaza Dance Studio*
*51 North Main St., on the plaza*
Aerobics and dance classes.

*The Tap School*                                                *482-3584*

*YMCA*                                                          *482-9622*
*1908 Ashland St. (Hwy. 66)*

*Yoga Center*                                                   *488-1231*
*416 Bridge St*

## GOLF

*Oak Knoll Public Golf Course*          *482-4311*
*3070 Highway 66*
Nine hole course, with possible expansion to eighteen under seemingly perpetual discussion; reservations taken; pro shop, carts and clubs available for rent; bar and restaurant.
There are three other public golf courses in the area:

*Bear Creek Golf Course, Medford*                               *773-1822*

*Cedar Links, Medford*                                          *773-4373*

*Laurel Hill Golf Course, Gold Hill*                            *855-7965*

And a private club that honors membership in other private clubs:

*Rogue Valley Country Club, Medford*                            *772-4050*

There are also tours organized to noted regional golf courses:

*NW Golf Tours* 482-9686
*345 Kent St.*

## HIKING

Mt. McLaughlin, off Highway 140 east of White City, provides the highest peak to climb in southern Oregon. Maps of the 5 mile trail from the parking lot to the 9495 ft. summit are available from the Forest Service. They have maps and information about other trails as well. The Pacific Coast National Scenic Trail passes through this area.

*Ashland Ranger Station* 482-3333
*645 Washington St.*

An outdoor class in eurhythmic dancing at the Normal School. *Southern Oregon Historical Society*

## HORSEBACK RIDING

*Painted Sky Stables* 488-0820
*2747 East Main St.*
Horseback riding, by the hour or overnight trips including meals.

## PARACHUTING

*Southern Oregon Sport
Parachute Center*                                    826-2004, 826-5389
Skydiving instruction

## RIVER TRIPS AND GUIDE SERVICES

*All Seasons Guide Service*                                    479-1081
*1360 Sunny Glen Way, Sunny Valley*
Trips on the Illinois River, best in the late spring.

*Ashland's Eagle Sun Inc.*                                    772-9910
*Box 873, Medford*
Paddle and oar boat trips lasting up to 5 days, also fishing trips.

*Briggs Rogue River Guide Service*          476-2941, 479-1504
*2750 Cloverlawn Drive, Grants Pass*
Rafting and fishing trips.

*Court's Whitewater Trips*          247-7033, 247-6676
*P.O. Box 1045, Gold Beach*
One day boat trips with a lunch stop in Paradise.

*Dale's Guide Service*                                    535-4918
*214 Cheryl #19, Phoenix*
Drift boat river fishing for salmon and steelhead on the Rogue, Chetco
and Elk Rivers.

*Echo River Trips*                                    415-652-1600
*6529 Telegraph Ave., Oakland CA*          800-652-3246 (CA)
One to five day Rogue river trips, in paddle or oar rafts. Other western
river trips also.

*Four Seasons Adventures*                                    482-8352
*290 Helman St., Ashland*
Oar, paddle or paddle assisted oar rafts, trips of all classes of difficulty,
lasting from half a day to a week, on the Klamath, Umpqua, Owhyee,
Rogue and several other western rivers. Complete recreation packages
for other outdoor enthusiasts, including fishermen.

*Galice Resort and Store Raft Trips*                    476-3818
*11744 Galice Rd, Merlin*

Half and full day Rogue River trips; self-guided raft tours also available.

> *Headwaters*                                                488-0583
> *P.O. Box 1086, Ashland*

Oar and paddle raft trips on the Klamath, Rogue and Umpqua Rivers, from a half to four days, from mild to wild; Kayak and fishing trips, too.

> *Hellgate Excursions*                                       479-7204
> *P.O. Box 982, Grant's Pass*

Two to five hour jet boat trips, some with stops for meals, on the Rogue.

> *Jerry's Rogue Jet Boats*                          247-7601, 247-4571
> *P.O. Box 1011, Gold Beach*

64 and 104 mile round trips on the Rogue River.

> *Jet Boat River Excursions*                                 582-0800
> *P.O. Box 658, Rogue River*

Two hour scenic trips or evening trips with dinner at the Rogue Riviera Restaurant.

> *Kingfisher Ltd.*                                           479-1468
> *14875 Galice Road, Merlin*

Spring and fall fishing trips.

> *Noah's World of Water*                                     488-2811
> *P.O. Box 11, Ashland*

Half day to five day trips in paddle rafts, inflatable kayaks and excursion rafts, on the Rogue, Klamath and Umpqua, at all levels. Drift boat fishing trips too.

> *Nomad Expeditions*                                         482-8433,
> *1940 Tolman Creek Rd., Ashland*                       415-334-5520

Half day to ten day rafting and kayaking trips on a variety of rivers, some available all year; three price levels, from cost cutting co-op style to trips with luxury accommodations in riverside lodges.

> *Northwest Drifters*                                        773-4782

Summer raft and kayak trips on the Rogue and Klamath Rivers plus fishing trips in the fall; both day trips and longer adventures with a combination of camp and lodge accommodations are offered.

*Otter River Trips*                                        *476-8590*
*P.O. Box 338, Merlin*

Half and full day fishing trips with all equipment provided, and white water raft trips, too.

*Orange Torpedo Trips, Inc.*            *479-5061, 479-2455*
*Grants Pass Float Co.*                    *773-7366 (Medford)*
*Box 1111, Grants Pass*

One and two day guided trips in oar rafts or inflatable kayaks (the orange torpedoes) on the Rogue, with elegant country inn accommodations on the overnight trips. Longer trips on other western rivers available.

*Outdoor Adventure River Specialists*          *476-3818*
*P.O. Box 614, Merlin*

Rafting.

*Paul Brooks Raft Trips*                              *476-8051*
*P.O. Box 638, Merlin, north of Grant's Pass*

Raft rentals, guided raft trips and kayaking on the Rogue; six hour trips with lunch and moonlight cruises.

*Pringle's Guide Service*                *772-2994, 535-3509*
*1570 Spring St., Medford*

Drift boat fishing and rafting.

*Professional River Fishing Guides*              *479-1765*
*142 Rogue Manor, Grants Pass*

Raft trips as well as fishing.

*River Adventure Float Trips*                        *476-6493*
*Box 841, Grants Pass*

Raft and fishing trips on the Rogue.

*River Trips Unlimited*                              *779-3798*
*4140 Dry Creek Rd., Medford*

Raft and kayak trips on the Rogue and Klamath Rivers, from one to four days; salmon and steelhead fishing trips.

*Rogue Canyon Guide Service*
*P.O. Box 1647, Grants Pass*

Fishing trips.

*Rogue Excursions Unlimited*         773-5983
*P.O. Box 855, Medford*

From one to four day trips, whitewater rafting or fishing for salmon or steelhead.

*Rogue Jet Boat Excursions*      476-2628, 476-6401
*953 S.E. Seventh St., Grants Pass*      800-334-4567
800-331-4567 (OR)

Two to five hour trips in hydrojet powered boats, some with meals.

*Rogue/Klamath Whitewater Co.*      772-8467
*1202 East Main St., Medford*

Paddle raft and fishing trips on the Rogue and Klamath Rivers, one half to two days, with various classes of rapids involved

*Rogue Rafting Co.*      878-2585
*Shady Cove, north of Medford on Hwy. 62*

Rafts rented for floating down a relatively gentle ten mile stretch of the river, with free shuttle service.

*Rogue Rider Raft Rental*      878-2326
*Shady Cove*

Free shuttle to the launch spot.

*Rogue River Mail Boat Trips*      247-7033, 247-6225
*P.O. Box 1165-G, Gold Beach*

Hydrojet powered boats on 64 to 104 mile trips, narrated by licensed pilots, with a two hour lunch break along the way. Special transportation to and from the boat and at all stops is provided for handicapped visitors.

*Rogue Wilderness, Inc.*      479-9554
*3388 Merlin Rd., Grants Pass*

One to four day raft and fishing trips on the Rogue, either camping out or staying in lodges overnight. Whitewater equipment rented and sold.

*Smith's River Adventures*      779-3708, 772-4652
*P.O. Box 4295, Medford*

One and two day raft and kayak trips on the Rogue and Klamath Rivers; one day salmon and steelhead fishing trips on the Rogue, too.

*Sundance Expeditions*      479-8508
*14894 Galice Rd., Merlin*

Raft and fishing trips; kayak sales and instruction.

*Whitewater Cowboys*                                        *479-0132*
*P.O. Box 481, Grants Pass*
Guided raft and fishing trips, raft rentals.

*Wilderness Waterways*                                      *758-3150*
*625 N.W. Starker, Corvallis*
Rafting on the Rogue, camping out or staying in rustic lodges.

*Wilderness World Raft Trips*
*3388 Merlin Rd., Merlin*

## ROLLER SKATING

*Medford Skate University*                                  *772-1400*
*2425 South Pacific Highway, Medford*
Rink with rentals, snack bar.

## ROWING

*Rowing/NW*                                       *482-2432, 482-2863*
*75 Dewey St.*
Instruction, shell rentals and sales.

## RUNNING

You won't lack company in Lithia Park and on the roads above it.
Races are scheduled in advance and listed in both the Chamber of
Commerce calendar and the Park Department flyer.

## SAILING

*Hobie House Marina*                                        *488-0595*
*Emigrant Lake*
Rent a sailboat, Hobie Cat or windsurfer for use on Emigrant or
Howard Prairie Lakes; Instruction available.

## SHOOTING

*Jackson County Sports Park*
*Kershaw Rd., off Hwy 140, 2 miles from White City*
Several ranges including a covered public sight-in range along with
other sports fields and facilities.

*Sportsman's Park*
*2 miles north on Frontage Rd. from the Merlin exit from I5*
A Josephine County Park specifically for shooting, with seven ranges and archery and hatchet throwing areas.

## SKIING

| | |
|---|---|
| *Ski Ashland* | *482-2897* |
| *8 miles from I-5 Mt. Ashland exit* | *482-4948, bus schedules* |
| | *482-2754, snow conditions* |

Open from the first skiable snow in late November through March, and weekends into April; Ski rentals, repairs and sales, instruction, cafeteria. Additional sources of rental equipment are listed on page 231.

There are cross country skiing areas at Lake of the Woods, Crater Lake, Fish Lake, Hyatt Lake and on Mt. Ashland. The Medford Chamber of Commerce offers maps of winter trails.

Inside the Sulphur Baths, circa 1910. *Ashland Public Library, print by Terry Skibby*

The required Oregon Sno-Park permits are available at the Department of Motor Vehicles office at I-5 exit #19, or at the Ski Ashland rental shop and offices.

## SOUTHERN OREGON STATE COLLEGE SPORTS FACILITIES

The swimming pool, tennis courts, weight room, racquetball courts, dance studio and gymnasium are open to the public at certain times for community classes, drop in basketball and volleyball games, and individual recreation. Schedules, and guest passes for which a small fee is charged, are available at the Physical Education Department, located in the section of the campus below Siskiyou Blvd. and Highway 66. For more information, call:

*Department of Physical Education*          482-6236

## SWIMMING

*Emigrant Lake*          776-7001
*Hwy. 66, just east of Ashland*
The swimming area is open daily in summer and the 270 foot, twin flume water slides should absorb a lot of youthful energy.

*Daniel Meyer Memorial Pool*          488-0313
*Hunter Park*
The schedule of when the pool is open to the public is available from the Park Department office. To find Hunter Park, turn east from Highway 66 onto Walker Ave. and then south on Homes. The pool, tennis courts and parking area are off Hunter Court.

*Jackson Hot Springs*          535-1555
*2253 Hwy. 99, Talent*
In summer the swimming pool and individual hot tubs are available to the public, but not at all times; call to check the schedule.

*SOSC pool*
The one indoor pool, operated year round; see above under Southern Oregon State College Facilities for details.

## TENNIS

Lighted courts are available at the following locations:

| | |
|---|---|
| *Lithia Park* | *2* |
| *Hunter Park* | *6* |
| *SOSC* | *8* |

There is no charge or reservation system for the courts in the city parks; for the college courts see above under SOSC. Big Al's tennis tournament is in July.

    *For information call:*                        *482-8796*

# *Miscellaneous Fun*

Some activities and attractions defy categorization but are none the less fun. Here is a list, from Arboretum to Zoo:

## ARBORETUM

*Southern Oregon Agricultural Experiment Station*
*569 Hanley Rd., Medford*                772-5165
There is an herb garden here,too, and research projects to see.

## BASEBALL

*Medford A's*                                770-5364
*Miles Field, on Highway 99 just south of Medford*
The Medford A's are a farm team of the Oakland A's; appearances by the Oakland team and Medford A's games with other Northwest League teams can be seen at Miles Field.

## FISH HATCHERY

*Cole Rivers Hatchery*                       878-2255
*Hwy. 62, Trail, near Lost Creek Dam*
The Oregon Fish and Game Commission operates the state's largest hatchery at Lost Creek Lake; telephone for information about tours.

## LLAMAS

*Juniper Ridge Ranch*                        482-9585
*9840 Mt. Ashland Rd.*

If you've always wanted an exotic pet that's also a good pack animal, call for an appointment to see the llamas raised here; they're for sale.

## OLD WEST

*Doubletree Ranch*                                          *476-2946*
*6000 Abegg Rd., Merlin*

Wagon tours; horseback rides and family style dinners; some of the boat trips on the Rogue stop here for a meal.

*Gold Gulch*                                                   *664-2847*
*Off I5, 10 miles north of Medford*

A replica of an old west mining town.

*Greensprings Box R Ranch*                      *482-1873*
*On Highway 66 east of Ashland*

A working cattle ranch with a living museum exhibit of pioneer artifacts. There are lodgings here (see page 163 ) and on some summer weekends, barbecues and square dances.

## POOL AND VIDEO GAMES

*SOSC Stevenson Union*                              *482-7151*
*Siskiyou Blvd. at Palm*

Open to the public in summer

*Goodtimes Family Restaurant*                 *482-4424*
*1951 Hwy. 66*

*The Bushes Hard Rock Burger Bar*             *482-3853*
*1474 Siskiyou Blvd.*

## SAWMILL TOUR

*Medford Corporation*                                 *773-7491*
*North Pacific Highway, Medford*

Self-guided tours of a sawmill and plywood mill.

## SLED DOG RACES

*The Southern Oregon Sled Dog Club*         *899-8698*

They sponsor races at Diamond Lake in February and March.

Shakespearean costume and entertainment help make the festival an experience to remember. *Oregon Shakespeare Festival, photo by Dwaine Smith.*

## TOURIST CLASSIC

*Oregon Vortex and House of Mystery*       *855-1543*
*4303 Sardine Creek Rd., Gold Hill, between Medford*
*and Grants Pass*
Peculiar physical phenomena are alleged to be visible here.

## TRAINS

*Medford Railroad Park*       *770-4586, 779-7979*
*Berrydale Ave. near Table Rock Rd.*
From I-5 take exit 30 onto Hwy. 62, the Crater Lake Highway, and

turn right on Table Rock Rd. at the Burger King. On the second and fourth Sundays of each month from April through October members of National Railway Historical Society and the Southern Oregon Live Steamers Club operate miniature steam trains over a mile of track that includes bridges, culverts and switching yards. Visitors can ride in the little cars and there is also a display of old railroad rolling stock (the real thing, not miniaturized).

## WILDLIFE PARKS

*Tigerville*                                              *846-7382*
*15200 Water Gap Rd., Williams, near Grants Pass*
Various big cats plus circus entertainment and refreshments.

*Wildlife Safari*                                         *679-6761*
*In Winston, near Roseburg, at exit 119 from I5*
Drive or ride a train through a park with exotic animals; there is a children's petting zoo, elephant rides, trained animal shows, and a restaurant.

# *Where to Stay*

Your choices in Ashland include two hotels, the traditional, high-rise Mark Antony, which is temporarily closed at this writing, and the smaller Columbia; fifteen motels ranging from tiny antiques like the ten unit Manor to deluxe modern giants like the Ashland Hills with 159 units; nearly thirty bed and breakfast inns of widely varying character; about sixteen short-term rental units ranging from tiny cottages to three bedroom houses; and a hostel. Campgrounds and parking for recreational vehicles can be found within a short distance of Ashland, along with more B & B's and rental units, and many more motels.

If you wait until you reach Main Street on a summer weekend, you won't have many choices, but you should still find something in town or close by. That is when the reservation services are invaluable. Twelve B&B's have formed a network whose slogan is "Nobody does it Bed-er." If none of their members has space, or you prefer a motel or hotel room, Sandy at Roomservice Reservations deals with a larger group of lodging places. She operates from 9 to 9 except Sundays and holidays, and there is no charge to you for her very effective services. She has twice found me excellent rooms late on a mid-season Friday afternoon.

| | |
|---|---|
| *Bed and Breakfast Network* | *482-2337* |
| *Roomservice Reservations* | *488-0338* |

If you are planning in advance you can consider the features that are important to you and aim for the place that best meets your needs. Among the things to think about are:

**Distance to restaurants and shopping and to the plays** — Does being able to walk everywhere, because you came without a car or just because you want to forget parking problems on your vacation, mean a lot to you? Any innkeeper who can possibly claim to be located within walking distance of something is likely to make some ambiguous claim in his or her brochures. All the lodgings that are less than a mile from the festival are listed by distance, below:

---

**Walking Home** — Lodging less than a mile from the corner of East Main and Pioneer:

**0 to .1 mile** *Columbia and Mark Antony — hotels*
*McCall House — B&B*
*Stone House — rentals*

**to .2 mile** *Bard's Inn — motel*
*Oak St. Station, Queen Anne, Stepsister,* Winchester Inn*— B&B's*
*B St. House, Spiridon House, Enders House — rentals*

**to .3 mile** *Main St. Inn, Cowslip's Belle, Gresham House Lithia Rose, Wisteria House — B&B's*
*Parkside Cottage — rentals*
*Ashland Youth Hostel*

**to .4 mile** *Stratford Inn — motel*
*Chanticleer, 455 B St, Edinburgh Lodge, RoyAl Carter House — B&B's*

**to .5 mile** *Bluebell House, Iris Inn, Woods House — B&B's*

**to .6 mile** *Manor Motel*
*Arden Forest Inn, Hersey House — B&B's*
*Auburn St. Cottage — rental*

**to .7 mile** *Ashland Guest Villa, Coach House, Miners Addition, Romeo Inn — B&B's*

**.9 mile** *Morical House — B&B*

---

There are some home truths about walking in Ashland that you need to know. First, it's hilly, and while walking down to town may seem delightful, hiking back up after an afternoon of shopping or a play may feel a lot harder. Second, it can get very hot in Ashland, over 100 degrees for days at a time, and though it's not humid, that sun is punishing. It also rains unpredictably. Third, the evening plays frequently last until

11:30, by which time more than a very short walk may not seem too appealing.

**Rates** — There isn't the precise relationship between facilities, luxury, or closeness to the festival and rates that it would seem reasonable to expect. Newer, more luxurious motels do charge more that the older, more Spartan ones, but bed and breakfast rates, as you will discover from the listings, are quite illogical.

The hills rising behind Ashland; the tall building on the left is the Mark Antony Hotel. *(Ashland Chamber of Commerce)*

111

Winter rates are substantially lower everywhere in Ashland, and some weekly rates are also available then. Rates are usually reduced, though not as drastically, during the spring and fall, particularly for midweek stays. If you are traveling in late spring or early fall, it could pay you to shop for a place that is not charging full summer rates.

If you are traveling alone there are also variations in rates that can affect your costs, but the single rooms available may be too cramped to be worth the small price difference. Some places also give discounts to seniors and AARP members, business travelers, and possibly other groups, for which you usually have to ask.

In the listings, the rates are quoted for two people in one room unless some other combination is specified. If you are quoted a rate drastically higher than those in the listing, higher than you are comfortable paying, try another place. There is a lot of competition for your business in Ashland, and no one inn has a monopoly on nice rooms. Rates are quoted without the 6% Ashland tax, with a few exceptions as noted, and rounded off to the nearest dollar in the few instances where a figure with cents is given by the management.

**Smokers, children and pets** — Motels and hotels permit smoking, though some now have non-smoking rooms which smell nicer to non-smoking guests. Bed and breakfast inns increasingly permit smoking only out of doors, on the porch or in the garden. If that would be a hardship for you, ask before reserving a room.

Children of all ages are welcome at hotels and motels, some of which have cribs and high-chairs available. Many B&B's set a lower limit on the age of child guests or discourage them entirely. The breakfasts do not include choices designed for children's tastes and the company often isn't prepared to talk appropriately with them either. I once endured a meal at an inn while another guest egged my daughter on to ever more detailed descriptions of what she had just learned in her first sex education class. 455 B Street, Bluebell House, Gresham Howe, The Iris Inn, Morical House and Oak Hill are prepared for small children; most others prefer them to be in their teens.

Taking pets traveling is not easy unless you're camping out or living in an RV. A few motels will take pets, some only with a damage deposit. Bed and breakfast inns are most unlikely to admit them.

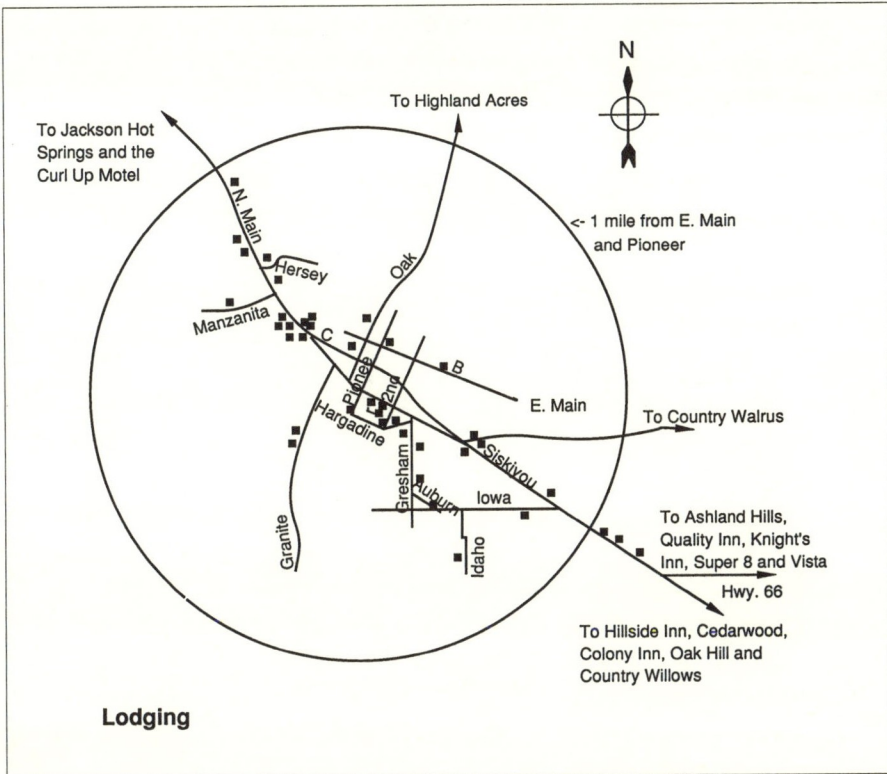

**Lodging**

**Handicapped access** — Individuals know best what special facilities they need, but in general, the larger motels, some of which have specially equipped rooms, are probably the best choices. The Mark Antony has an elevator, but tiny bathrooms, some up a step from the rooms, could cause problems for wheelchairs. A few bed and breakfast inn's have level entries and main floor rooms that might work out for some handicapped visitors, the RoyAl Carter House for one. A detailed discussion with the individual innkeeper would be the only way to determine if the room would be suitable. The two newest B&B's, Arden Forest and Oak Hill, have both announced their intention to provide rooms that are wheelchair accessible.

In reviewing all these lodging places I have discounted special circumstances that affected my enjoyment of a particular motel or inn but would not be likely to be repeated for other visitors. I have tried to provide factual information to help you sort through the various brochures and advertisements. The success of a vacation should not

113

depend on the traveler's ability to decode puffery and detect what hasn't been said. It isn't nice to learn, only after arriving, that some important item has been left out of the brochure or that you forgot to ask about some feature vital to your enjoyment of your visit.

# Hotels and Motels

About three quarters of the guest lodgings in Ashland are motel rooms, and there's no shortage any more; even at the height of the summer season there is usually space at one of the big new places near the freeway. The only trouble with motel rooms is that they don't seem very festive — they're what you get when you can't drive any more, and you don't always get tired where there's a good one. If you're going to spend a vacation based in a motel, as opposed to crashing for a few hours before continuing a trip, it's worth finding one that pleases you, or at least is thoroughly comfortable.

I have either stayed at or inspected rooms in all the motels and hotels listed in the following section. I've tried to describe each place objectively, giving facts that aren't always in the brochures and pointing out potential problems as well as mentioning what I liked. Of course, you may not be bothered by noise, which drives me wild, and may loathe the sort of funky old place that has a nostalgic charm for me, so I have not tried to establish any kind of rating system with numbers of stars, or little beds, to guide you.

Unless otherwise noted in the individual listings, all hotel and motel rooms will have a private bath, a color television with satellite or cable service, a direct dial phone on which you can make local and credit card calls at no charge, and an individually controlled air conditioning unit. Motels and hotels also normally provide parking for your car, have a swimming pool and take major credit cards. Other facilities and services, such as kitchens or room-service meals will be listed where they are available.

If you want your pick of places you do need to reserve in advance. If you need room for a crowd, or plan to walk to everything, or want to pay a bargain price, you should reserve early, probably as soon as you order tickets. Those are just the places that people return to, year after year, and they fill up first. And for maximum comfort, you should find out where your room is going to be. Top floor rooms facing away from traffic are usually quietest, and if you dislike basements, you should avoid those ground floor rooms that are sunk below ground level and look out at retaining walls or the backs of the shrubbery. Ask, and if the person taking your reservation isn't cooperative about helping you choose a room you'll enjoy, try another motel.

The descriptions of the motels and hotels are listed in alphabetical order. To help you decide which places are worth further investigation, here is a list arranged by price:

---

### MOTEL RATES

For a double room in high season, 1987-88:

| | |
|---|---|
| Vista Motel | $ 22 - 30 |
| Jackson Hot Springs | 25 - 30 |
| Manor Motel | 30 - 42 |
| Knight's Inn | 30 - 42 |
| Palm Motel | 32 - 44 |
| Ashland Motel | 33 - 47 |
| Columbia Hotel | 35 - 48 |
| Hillside Inn | 37 - 55 |
| Curl Up Motel | 38 - 42 |
| Timbers Motel | 38 - 54 |
| Super 8 Motel | 40 - 42 |
| Valley Entrance Motel | 40 - 54 |
| Cedarwood Motel | 44 - 56 |
| Flagship Quality Inn | 50 - 60 |
| Ashland Hills Inn | 50 - 80 |
| Mark Antony | 55 70 |
| Stratford Inn | 57 |
| Bard's Inn | 65 - 80 |

---

*Ashland Hills Inn*                              *482-8310*
*Windmill Inns of America*          *1-800-452-5315 (OR)*
*2525 Ashland St., at I-5 exit #14*     *1-800-547-4747 (USA)*

Ashland Hills is the top of the line. If it were next to Lithia Park and a little less garishly decorated, there would be no question where to stay. As it is, off by the freeway interchange and decorated in exuberant motel-ugly, it is still outstandingly comfortable, with a genuinely caring staff and unmatched facilities. There is a full restaurant and cocktail lounge in the complex as well as a pool and spa, tennis courts and areas for playing horseshoes and volleyball. There is room service and you can order an elaborate picnic to take to a Britt concert. There are non-smoking rooms here and ones equipped for the handicapped. And if the decor inside seems excessive, the landscaping outside is attractively lush and cool.

The individual rooms range from big to huge. An economy room on the outside (that is, not one they classify and charge for as a view room) had in fact a lovely view of the hills from its balcony. Since all the rooms open off central halls the view could be enjoyed with no loss of privacy. The furnishings included a queen size bed, night tables with lamps, a table with two upholstered chairs, a straight chair, and one of those all-purpose bureau/desk/TV/luggage pieces found only in motels. With all of this there was open space. The bath was large, tiled and well equipped.

The nominal cost of this room was $50 for one or two people, but Ashland Hills has more rooms than all the bed and breakfast places in Ashland put together. That explains both why it's hard to get a room in a B&B and why the Ashland Hills management offers incentives to get business. Even in the summer they give AARP discounts, discounts for return visitors, commercial rates (show your business card) and may well give other breaks for which its worth asking. In winter they cut this rate in half. The summer rates for other rooms range up to $80, up to $200 for suites.

Upon registering I was asked what time in the morning I would like my complimentary coffee, or tea or decaf, and newspaper. In the room I found a long list of other free services, including the use of an iron and ironing board, first aid supplies, bicycles, transportation to and from the plays, and many more. There are mints in the room and a basket of apples in the lobby. And there are a few negatives in addition to the location, principally the noise, not from the freeway which is remarkably inaudible, but from all the other air conditioners, so that leaving the doors to the balcony open while you sleep is not practical even though they are screened. There are also some rooms on the ground floor that are partially below grade and may seem basementy, though I have not been in them to know for sure.

The reservation service put me at Ashland Hills because it was all that was available on a summer weekend. If the same thing happens to you, prepare to be pleasantly surprised.

*Ashland Motel*                                            *482-2561*
*1145 Siskiyou, at Garfield, near SOSC*

The architecture here is a fantastic combination of Elizabethan half-timbering, Old West false fronts and those blue glass windows favored in hot valley towns before air conditioning. It may sound like a neat synthesis of town and festival but it looks pretty peculiar. The buildings, part one storey and part two, face a large, hot parking area with the swimming pool in the middle.

The Oregon Hotel; note the boardwalk. *Southern Oregon Historical Society*

118

The Ashland is an older motel that is far from fancy but seems well maintained. Rooms for one or two persons range from a very small unit for $33 to a two room suite with three beds for $56, with most costing somewhere in between $43 and $47. And there are the usual winter reductions. All the rooms are quite basic, though equipped with the necessities, including phones and air conditioners, and some of them have kitchens. The management is very friendly, the pool is full of kids and visitors happily return year after year.

| *Bard's Inn, Best Western* | *482-0049* |
| *132 North Main, just off the plaza* | *1-800-528-1234* |

Bard's Inn is the closest motel to the festival, and it has some very good features: baths with forceful showers and windows for light and fresh air, light-proof curtains, air conditioners in the rear walls so front windows can be open without hearing everyone else's unit, handsome views of the hills from the upper rooms. It also has new owners who have refurbished both the rooms and the exterior with handsome results. Outside there is fresh paint and blue mansard roof detailing and inside, new oak furniture with fabrics in soft, cool colors. If looks were all a motel needed, Bard's Inn would be hard to fault.

Unfortunately, there still are faults, some of which may be impossible for the new management to correct. The worst is noise. The cars on Main Street are there, but not as loud as you might expect — the rooms face away from the street, and the restaurant forms a partial shield. But conversation from other rooms and from people on the walkways is all too audible, even with the windows closed. There is also a refrigerator in each room which makes refrigerator noises; what you never notice by day in your kitchen sounds awfully loud in the middle of the night, though if you don't need ice, you can turn it off.

The parking shortage is also aggravating. The motel has acquired two lots across the street, one on North Main and one on Helman, but they're not ideally close to the rooms, especially if you're alone and it's late, or you have heavy suitcases. The office also closes very early, between 10 and 11 PM; once it's closed you can't reach any of the motel staff for help nor can you receive incoming phone calls.

In spite of these problems, Bard's Inn is an exceptionally convenient place to stay if you want motel amenities. It has them all for from $65 to

$80 for two, the top price being a two room suite, and it's close to some of the best breakfasts in town.

*Cedarwood Inn;*                                                          *488-2000*
*1801 Siskiyou, beyond the Hwy. 66 turnoff*     *1-800-547-4141*

Though new, this is a rather Spartan motel with moderate prices. Small singles go for $34, larger rooms for $44 to $56. The rooms are plainly furnished and have fixed windows with only a small sliding section that opens. The plan is unusual: in addition to the usual three storeys of rooms in a straight section facing the street, another group of rooms is built facing into a small, deep courtyard. The upper rooms at the back of the straight section ought to be pleasantly light and have a view of the hills. The rooms on the front are very close to the parking lot and the traffic, and some on the ground floor are partially below grade, with windows at ground level.

The Cedarwood has the usual phones and television and air conditioning. Suites and rooms with wet bars or kitchenettes are available, and there are also saunas for the guests, and according to the plan, a billiard room. The Cedarwood's claim to distinction is two pools, one outdoors and only solar heated, and a heated one covered by a dome. This pool and its enclosure take up most of the courtyard, creating an unpleasantly dark and crowded feeling in the surrounding rooms, especially on the lower floor.

The Cedarwood is way out on Siskiyou by itself, well south of most of the restaurants in town. The restaurant and bar at the motel were scheduled to reopen in late 1987 as a branch of Bee Gee's, a popular Medford family restaurant with a standard coffee shop menu and very reasonable prices. The motel staff is friendly and cooperative, and though not glamorous, the rooms are good value for a new motel.

*Columbia Hotel*                                                         *482-3726*
*262 1/2 East Main, between 2nd and 3rd*

The Columbia advertises itself as a little European Hotel, and indeed, it is above a line of stores, with only a doorway and a smart, striped awning at street level. Also in the European tradition, some of the rooms lack a private bath. These rooms range from $35 to $40; those with private bath cost $48. Rooms on the front have huge windows overlooking Main Street; the view is pleasant but the traffic noise and street lamps are

The same hotel in the late 1920's with a new name and a new look. The First Interstate Bank occupies this block today. *Ashland Public Library, print by Terry Skibby*

bothersome. Rooms at the back open onto light wells or the parking area, but are quieter.

Location is the Columbia's prime asset — it's a short walk to the festival, or any of the in-town restaurants. Modern hotel amenities are mostly lacking. The only telephone is an old fashioned booth in the lobby, but it's the kind with a seat and a door you can close, and at least you're not outside with the traffic roaring by. There are some television sets but without cable and of course, there is no pool. There is also no elevator and therefore no handicapped access.

Unlike most of the self-consciously antique bed and breakfast places, the Columbia feels genuinely old. The ceilings are high, there are original bathroom fixtures, and the furniture is what was typical of hotels fifty years ago. It all feels pretty worn out, too, with burns on bureau tops and limp curtains. The management seems to be gradually repairing and replacing things, and it's very clean, but it isn't elegant — in a way that's its charm.

121

*Curl Up Motel*                                         *482-4700*
*50 Lowe Road, at I-5 exit #19*            *1-800-447-4701 (OR),*
                                                              *1-800-482-4701 (USA)*

Exit 19 is the first Ashland turn off going south or the third going north; if you went past the motel you would end up just north of Ashland. As a charming location from which to attend the festival this doesn't look promising — just a standard, out of the box motel, curled up in the arms of the freeway, with only the local DMV office and a couple of gas stations for company.

The rooms, however, are surprisingly comfortable. The furnishings and decoration are fairly luxurious and very clean. The noise level inside is quite low, though this is achieved in part with sealed windows. Ventilation is through the modern air conditioning/heating units. On the down side, there is no pool.

Prices here range from $34 for one or $38 for two in one queen bed to $42 for a two bed room. Non-smoking rooms, complimentary coffee, and not least, a very pleasant, accommodating manager, make this a nicer place than it would first appear to be.

*Flagship Quality Inn*                                   *488-2330*
*2520 Ashland St., at I-5 exit #14*            *800-228-5151*

The first impression, driving through the half-timbered gateway of the Flagship, is that they have tried to reproduce a galleried Elizabethan Inn, with balcony walkways and multi-paned windows. Of course, the detailing is not at all exact, and the courtyard is lacking one side, but it does seem an appropriate idea for a town so involved with Shakespeare.

The rooms at the Flagship are large and luxuriously furnished by motel standards, and the compartmented bath/dressing areas are convenient. Most rooms here look toward the parking lot and swimming pool, rather than at the freeway, so they should be reasonably quiet, though external walkways are noisier than central halls and there isn't much greenery to muffle car sounds. Rates range from $50 to $60 for rooms for one or two people, to $72 and $82 for two room suites with kitchens.

A breakfast of fruit, rolls and coffee is laid out in the office for guests to help themselves. Like the Ashland Hills across the street, the Flagship has a free shuttle to take guests to the plays. And in addition to the usual amenities, all rooms here have a decorative fireplace and a second phone in the bathroom, features whose usefulness you may question.

The basic rooms and rates at the Flagship are comparable to those across the street at the Ashland Hills, but the atmosphere is quite different. The Ashland Hills feels like a hotel or resort, with big public spaces and many extra services. The Flagship feels like a superior motel, with a small office and a twenty-four hour coffee shop next door.

*Hillside Inn*                    482-2626
*1520 Siskiyou, just past the turnoff onto Hwy. 66*

This seems like the oldest unreconstructed auto court still operating, in Ashland and maybe anywhere, but it's about to change. The little cabins among the trees, with their covered parking spaces in between, are scheduled to be replaced. It's not hard to understand that maintaining these museum pieces has become too much for the owners; it's just sad to see something so nostalgic disappear.

There are already newer units at the Hillside, pleasant looking groups of rooms surrounding the pool and patio, turning away from the street and its traffic noise. When I visited, guests were swimming and eating brunch at tables on the patio and clearly enjoying the sheltered intimacy this arrangement promotes. The rates for two people presently range from $37 to $55 and kitchens are available for an additional $8, though this will change when the least expensive units go. These are rates for cash payment; credit cards are accepted but the 3% charged to the motel by the card companies is passed on to the guest here.

One of the nicest features of the Hillside Inn is its woodsy setting; the cars have room to park, but somehow there isn't that central area of hot asphalt that makes so many motels oppressive. I hope, when the newest units are built, that this won't be lost. My other concern is with the Hillside's neighbors; The Bushes Hard Rock Burger Bar advertises that they stay open until 3 AM, which could be noisy, and a Dairy Queen is being built next door. At least the new units are going to be built at the rear of the property, not next to the Dairy Queen.

*Jackson Hot Springs*                    535-155
*2253 Hwy 99, Talent*

Although it isn't in Ashland, Jackson Hot Springs is about the same distance north as the freeway interchange motels — Ashland Hills, Flagship, Vista — are south. Going north from Ashland on North Main Street it is on the left, about two and one half miles from the festival. If

123

you are on I-5, take exit #19 toward Ashland and turn right on Hwy. 99; you will see the sign almost immediately on your left.

Hot springs and mineral water were important in Ashland's development, though the grand resorts were only planned, never built. Jackson Hot Springs has the waters but absolutely no grandeur. In fact, you need to be entertained by funky old places to stay here.

The rooms here are ancient cabins with baths and kitchens for $25 (one double bed) or $30 (two double beds). The floors aren't level, and the furnishings could be duplicated from your local Salvation Army store, but the rooms look clean enough, and the old fashioned, rural feeling has a certain charm. The cabins are not air conditioned, though most are shaded by big trees, and not all have television.

The large public swimming pool is free for guests and mineral baths in private tubs are available for $5 for 1 1/2 hours; massages can also be arranged. There is tent camping on a large grassy area and RV parking is also available here.

### Knight's Inn Motel                                        482-5111
*2359 Highway 66, at I-5 exit #14, on the Ashland side of I-5*

The Knight's Inn is a middle aged motel, middling in its level of luxury, too. There is a two storey building facing the highway traffic and a one storey section forming an L. Parking and the swimming pool occupy the space in between — a very typical configuration, unfortunately without much greenery to soften it in this case.

Rates here are quite modest: $27 for one person to $42 for two people in the best room. There are no kitchens or suites or other frills, and no charm at all, but no obvious problems either, except for the noise level that comes with a freeway interchange location.

### Manor Motel                                             482-2246
*476 North Main, about 6 blocks north of the plaza*

The Manor Motel is another antique, but in this case it has been lovingly maintained, recently repainted in cheerful gray and red, and attractively landscaped. There is no swimming pool here except for a little pond for the ducks who live in the shaded picnic area. There are also no phones. The office will take messages and there is a pay phone outside Big Al's, next door.

The rooms here are simply but adequately furnished, have television and air conditioning, and some have refrigerators or kitchens. Because most of the windows do not face the street it is pleasantly quiet in spite of the North Main traffic, and the restaurant next door closes early.

The low rates make the Manor something of a best buy for lodging this close to the center of town, though it's a long walk if it's hot or you're not young anymore. Rates range from $28 for one to $75 for nine in a four room suite with a kitchen. A list detailing the facilities and price for each unit is available.

### *Mark Antony Hotel*       482-1721
### *212 East Main*

You can't miss the only sky-scraper in town; just two blocks from the Festival, it towers over everything else. The deco facade and grand, old-fashioned lobby suggest that rehabilitating and reopening it a few years ago was a happy choice. Half the ground floor is a popular cocktail lounge, the Stage Door, and at night people also sit in the lobby half to enjoy the pianist in the dining area. Among the hotel's other assets are a convenient parking lot and a swimming pool.

Unfortunately, like skin deep beauty, the Mark Antony's elegance is only lobby high. The rooms, when the one ancient elevator finally gets you to your floor, are small and bleak. The furnishings of one room consisted of a bed, a dressing table and a portable television on a tea cart, no pictures or decoration of any kind, no chairs or tables. Air conditioners have been installed in the lower halves of the windows by bolting them to the sash so that, except for the few rooms with two windows, there is no fresh air available without running the noisy machine, and possibly even worse, the conditioners block the beautiful view.

Ever since it was reopened the Mark Antony has had financial problems and it closed once again in the fall of 1987. When it reopens for the 1988 season the rates will be $55 to $70. The location is as good as you can get, right in the middle of the shopping and restaurant area and an easy walk to the plays, but the rooms are truly minimal.

### *Palm Motel*       482-2636
### *1065 Siskiyou Blvd., near SOSC*

This is a small motel, older but well maintained, the sort that used to be called an auto court. Lots of lawn and big trees plus a pool make it attractive in hot weather. The units are pleasant, if simply decorated, and are equipped with air conditioners and color cable television. There is a wide range of size and price here, from a basic room with one double bed, for $32, to a two bedroom and kitchen unit that sleeps up to five and rents for $54. ($27 to $42 in winter). Cribs and high chairs are available without charge.

The worst thing here is the lack of telephones. The office will take messages, but you have to return your calls from an open pay phone with the Siskiyou traffic thundering by. Traffic noise may also be a problem in some of the rooms nearest to the road, though the pool and lawn area, and the office, form a partial barrier.

In addition to these units the motel manages five two and three bedroom houses which are listed as rentals. If you ask, they will give you a list, both of the units and the houses, with details of the number and sizes of beds in each room and which units have kitchens. The Palm is a very friendly place with a devoted clientele of repeat visitors; the owners are right to boast of the woman who has been coming for thirty-five years to stay a week in the same unit.

> *Stratford Inn*                               *488-2151*
> *555 Siskiyou Blvd., at Sherman St.*      *1-800-453-5319 (OR)*
>                                        *1-800-547-4741 (USA)*

The Stratford Inn claims to be a four block walk to the festival; I think it might seem like a long four blocks in hot weather or late at night, though ordinarily it's not an impossible distance. It's located near the beginning of Siskiyou, where the two directions of traffic separate onto East Main and Lithia Way, and if you're looking for it, the blue roof is unmistakable.

After the blue roof, the first thing you notice driving up to the Stratford is the indoor swimming pool behind the big windows. If you look more closely you will notice the clever panels that hide the air conditioners and the way the three storey building has been set somewhat below grade to minimize its height. The Stratford presents a handsome face to the street and hides its parking lot in back.

The rooms, which open off long central corridors, are large but quite plain. The current rate is $57 for two in a room with either one or two queen size beds. Kitchens are available for an additional $15 to $20 and some rooms have sofa beds for additional guests. There are also special units here for the handicapped.

The Stratford offers a number of amenities including ski lockers, morning coffee and covered parking spaces. The front units are fairly close to the noisy street, and in the case of some on the ground floor, quite subterranean in feeling, but the rooms are basically comfortable and the location is excellent.

*Super 8 Motel*                                            482-8887
*2350 Ashland St, near I-5 exit #14*            1-800-843-1991

Super 8 Motels are a chain of independently owned franchises with the stated policy of providing "the basics you need for a good night's sleep...and low rates." The Ashland Super 8 is a severely plain building with three floors of rooms reached from central hallways. Rooms with one queen bed overlook the parking lot and cost $37 for one or $40 for two; rather nicer rooms with two queen beds have a view of trees and cost $42. Suites with a sofa and a wet bar cost $46.

The overall impression of this motel is that nothing was wasted on frills, yet a number of frills are offered: an indoor pool, Showtime movies, free coffee in the lobby. There is also a guest laundry, an unusual and potentially very convenient feature. There are non-smoking and handicapped-equipped rooms available here, too. It almost seems as if the design purposely lacks charm in order to convey the budget message — it's nicer than it looks.

*Timbers Motel*                                            482-4242
*1450 Ashland St., just below Siskiyou Blvd.*

Attractive brown and white, two storey buildings step up the sloped site and form a sheltered L here, with the office, pool and landscaping shielding the units from the street. The Timbers is not the newest or oldest motel, nor the most or least luxurious one. It's a truly happy medium.

The range of units available includes singles for which the charge is $34, two bed rooms which cost $38, or $48 with a kitchen, and two room family units with three beds for $54. The rooms have all the standard features and are attractive though not too big. The bathrooms have windows, which is nice for both light and ventilation. Also, the air conditioners are located at the rear of the units so you don't hear them if you choose to open your windows in front.

The Timbers is a comfortable place to stay and very good value at these rates. The two neighboring restaurants, Papa D's (pizza) and the Golden Dynasty (Chinese), don't open until lunchtime, but it's not far to Andre's if you like to breakfast close by.

| | |
|---|---|
| *Valley Entrance Motel* | *482-2641* |
| *1193 Siskiyou Blvd., opposite SOSC* | *1-800-626-6100 (OR),* |
| | *1-800-547-6414 (USA)* |

If you stay here you are bound to meet the owner. His hands-on management style includes registering guests, filling coffee cups in the restaurant (Andre's), and being around all the time to see that everything is done right. He's a good source of local history too.

Until recently the Valley Entrance was a small, older motel. Those units are still there, but the new, three storey building is larger and more luxurious. Rooms with one queen bed cost from $40 to $48, ones with a king bed or two queens are $50 to $54, and larger units with two bedrooms and beds for up to six people are also available.

Rooms in the new section are nearly as luxuriously furnished as those at the Ashland Hills Inn, though the baths are smaller and the exterior walkways make the rooms less private. Those on the rear of the building are very quiet, and even the front units are well back from the street and at least partly sheltered by the restaurant building. As seems to be typical of recently built motels, some of the ground floor units are partially below ground level here.

In addition to the standard motel amenities — pool, phones, air conditioning — room service meals are available here. You can order anything on the Andre's menu at the modest cost of $1 per person over the menu price.

| | |
|---|---|
| *Vista Motel* | *482-4423* |
| *535 Clover Lane, at I-5 exit # 14* | |

This is a very modest, concrete block motel, located behind the Shell Station, but it appears to be quite clean and the people running it are certainly pleasant. Rates range from $22 to $30, which makes these the cheapest rooms in town. The units have television and air conditioning and there is even a tiny swimming pool. Freeway noise may be a problem for some people — you're quite close — and there are no room phones.

The Vista is not on the standard tourist lists; it may be possible to get a room here when the other inexpensive places are full.

# Bed and Breakfast Inns

Bed and breakfast is the latest travel fashion, and there are more B&B's in Ashland than in many, much larger cities. These days whole books are published rhapsodizing about the new inns in various scenic areas, and escaping to the country to run one seems to be the current yuppie dream. Reality, for both guest and innkeeper, is sometimes less idyllic.

Close to a quarter of the inns in Ashland are on the market or have changed hands recently. The prices of those actively listed with realtors in the fall of 1987 ranged from $149,000 to $395,000. The significance of this to potential guests is twofold. For one thing, new hosts can mean a new style of operation, possibly more to your taste, possibly less. For another, paying a big mortgage with the rent from a few rooms may require charging much higher rates.

I have stayed at almost all the bed and breakfast inns in Ashland, and those which never had an empty room when I was there, I have visited, inspecting rooms if they weren't yet occupied and talking to the innkeepers. I wanted to experience the intangibles of these unique places, the feeling that basically comes from the hosts' concepts of their inns and from their personal interaction with their guests. I wanted to eat their breakfasts, not just read their descriptions. I can describe the physical situation, the beds and baths and breakfasts, and I can try to suggest the nature of my experience, but the personality of each inn is only half of an equation which each guest will complete differently.

Bed and Breakfast Inns are highly variable in style and amenities but it's safe to assume that you won't have either a telephone or a television set — I've noted the exceptions in the listings. There is usually a telephone in the common areas that is available to guests for local or credit card calls, but it usually isn't very private and you can't tie up the line for long bouts of business phoning. TV sets don't fit in the antique ambiance most B&B's strive for, and it can be frustrating when major news breaks and no set is available. If World War III threatens when you are in an Ashland B&B, you may have to ask the hosts if you can watch the news with them; I'm sure they allow the twentieth century into their private quarters.

Air conditioning varies in B&B's; some have individual room units, others have central systems, which are much quieter but can't be adjusted by individual guests, and a few still have no cooling at all, though the trend is toward installing it. In order to get a license innkeepers have to provide off-street parking for guests; it is often located at the rear of the garden, off the alleys which bisect most blocks in the older parts of town. Swimming pools are rarely found at B&B's and few of them take credit cards. What B&B's do have, what makes then unique, are porches and decks, and living and dining rooms, where you can get to know your hosts and your fellow guests.

A word about breakfasts: It's delightful to come downstairs to a home cooked meal instead of braving the crowds in order to eat coffee shop food, but you have to enjoy taking what you are served since there are usually no choices. Most hosts ask when you arrive if you have food allergies and what you like to drink, and whether the scheduled time will work for you, but that still doesn't give the flexibility of a restaurant.

The difference between a full breakfast and a continental one seems trivial to me. An Ashland continental breakfast usually consists of both fresh fruit and fruit juice, a selection of baked goods, butter, real jam (not in plastic packs), and your choice of coffee, decaf or tea. Full breakfasts have one or more hot things added to this list, typically egg dishes like quiche or eggs benedict. Either way, you won't starve.

It's the style of presentation that makes the biggest difference in B&B breakfasts. At one extreme, the ingredients for a breakfast are delivered to your room for you to prepare and eat in solitude. At the other, everyone gathers around one big table for an hour or more of food and conversation. Some hosts cook your eggs individually and spend most of their time in the kitchen while others do make-ahead dishes so they can join the guests in the dining room. In some inns there are separate tables, or a long period during which breakfast is served, so that guests tend to eat in small groups. And occasionally you will be the only guest, which is a good chance to get to know your hosts.

And about the unmentioned B, baths: We Americans have learned to cope with shared baths in Europe. We come back and brag about the money we saved and the Europeans we met by avoiding the tourist hotels. Most bed and breakfast inns have been created in houses that were designed for families and built before baths were commonplace. Shared baths, or baths which are assigned for the use of one room's guests but don't open off that room, are sometimes the best the innkeeper could devise without ruining the old house charm that B&B lovers look for.

The bathroom issue isn't one of lines forming in the morning or mad dashes down the hall as in those old movies where a big family struggles to survive the depression. I've seldom had to wait, even where several rooms shared one bath, but you can't steam the wrinkles out of a dress or let your washing drip over a tub that you share. And while an assigned bath somewhere down the hall works for doing your laundry, people who need to get up in the middle of the night can find this arrangement inconvenient, particularly if the route involves going up and down stairs or through the living room.

Bath sharing can be made more palatable by the innkeeper. A rack of fingertip towels means guests don't have to remember to bring hand towels on every visit. A stack of bath mats avoids having to share a damp, communal one. And if bath towels are also stored in the bathroom, to be discarded in a hamper after one use, then they needn't be carried to and from your room. You should ask where the bath is if sharing or having it away from the bedroom is not acceptable.

You also should ask about the room's location when reserving space at an inn. In B&B's on busy streets, as with motels, ask for a room at the rear if noise bothers you. Main floor rooms that open directly off the living area can feel very exposed and noisy compared to traditional upstairs bedrooms. Rooms in outbuildings can be the quietest, but they often lack the architectural interest of the main house and may feel remote from the life of the inn. If you call early enough to have a choice of rooms, most innkeepers will be happy to describe what they have available. The occasional harried host will say, "Well, one's pink and one's blue; take your choice," but most are pleased to discuss their inn and eager to make your stay a success.

Again, before the alphabetical listings, a list arranged by price:

| 1988 BED AND BREAKFAST RATES | | | |
|---|---|---|---|
| **IN ASHLAND:** | | Highland Acres | $ 65 -*80 |
| RoyAl Carter | $ 44 -*60 | Morical House | 70 |
| Wisteria House | 45 -*65 | Hersey House | 70 - 75 |
| Coach House | 49 | Country Willows | 75 - 85 |
| Country Walrus(s) | 55 | Gresham House | 78 |
| Miners Addition | 55 | Chanticleer | 79 - *130 |
| 455 B Street (s) | 55 - 60 | Romeo Inn | 84 - *138 |
| Woods House | 55 - 70 | Winchester Inn | 89 |
| Bluebell House | 58 - 65 | | |
| McCall House (s) | 58 - 68 | **OUTSIDE OF ASHLAND** | |
| Iris Inn (s) | 60 | Jacksonville Inn | $ 50 |
| Main Street Inn | 60 | Treon's Homestay (s) | 50 |
| Oak Street(s) | 60 | The Farm House | 55 |
| Arden Forest | 60 -*68 | Reames House | 55 |
| Cowslip's Belle | 60 - 70 | Shutes Lazy S | 55 |
| Guest Villa | 64 | Mt. Ashland Inn | 60-70 |
| Step Sister | 64 | Tou Velle House (s) | 65 |
| Edinburgh Lodge | 65 | McCully House | 65-70 |
| Lithia Rose (s) | 65 | Greenwood Tree | 65-*75 |
| Oak Hill | 65 | Neil Creek House | 75 |
| The Queen Anne | 65 - 70 | Livingston Mansion | 80 |
| (s) shared bath | | *suite | |

*Arden Forest Inn*                                        *488-1496*
*261 W. Hersey St.*

Ashland's newest B&B opened during the winter of 1987-88. West Hersey Street, which is east of (below) North Main, is an unpaved farm road. Just a block from highway traffic and city houses is a group of old farmhouses, one of which has been renovated as Arden Forest Inn. The area is an enchanted island out of the rural past. I hope the new inn can maintain that feeling, in spite of the building code's strict requirements; it was still under construction when I saw it.

The host, a designer whose studio is located here too, plans to have a variety of accommodations with twin and queen beds. Rooms are now available with private baths at $60, including a full breakfast, and a two room suite is $68. Rooms accessible to the handicapped are also planned.

### Ashland Guest Villa (The Lambs)        488-1508
634 Iowa Street, two blocks above Siskiyou

The Ashland Guest Villa is one of the first bed and breakfast inns to open here. The brochure describes it as a "fabulous 50's redwood mansion…just two blocks from downtown." It's a nice, big house, but mansion is stretching a bit, and it is two blocks from a point on Siskiyou Blvd. that's well beyond the downtown shops and restaurants. Four rooms rent for $64 and have unusual amenities, according to the brochure: air conditioning, color TV and telephones.

My only unpleasant experience with an Ashland innkeeper occurred when I arrived here. The owner denied any knowledge of my reservation and turned me away. My check, which she eventually returned, may have been delayed in the mail, but I had given her my name and number when I called. This kind of treatment could ruin a vacation, so if you decide to stay here, do be sure to get written confirmation of your reservation.

### Ashland's Main Street Inn        488-0969
142 North Main, two doors north of Bard's Inn

Another of Ashland's pioneer bed and breakfast inns, Main Street is for people who don't like the social breakfast table or hanging around with the hosts. You are greeted nicely, shown your room, and then, unless you knock and ask for something, your hosts are invisible.

Breakfast arrives on an electric cart that is parked outside your door before you get up. You wheel it in when you want it, plug it in and the coffee maker and bun warmer do their jobs. My tray had a carafe of genuine, freshly squeezed orange juice, a lovely ripe peach with a sharp knife for peeling it, and cinnamon bread in the warmer — an altogether delicious meal but delivered by unseen hands and eaten in solitude.

The inn is a grand old Victorian with high ceilings and big rooms. I counted twelve pieces of furniture in my room and there was lots of unoccupied floor space. The furnishings are a comfortable mixture of old but not antique pieces and the decor is homey — no overpowering decorator elegance here. Each room is equipped with a color television set (no cable), a refrigerator, and a lock on the door. The central air conditioning is reasonably effective and quiet. Two rooms have double

Creative recycling of buildings is nothing new; the Vendome Hotel, which stood on East Main opposite the library, was originally a public school. *Ashland Public Library*

beds and one has three singles; one has a private bath and two have assigned baths at the other end of the hall. All cost $60 ($49 in winter) for two.

The Main Street Inn is a very comfortable place to stay with one serious problem. The Main Street traffic sounds like it is going to drive over your pillow. It may be because the inn is located just at the top of a little rise, or perhaps because it lacks double glazing, but the noise in all three rooms is extraordinarily loud, even with the windows closed.

*Bluebell House*                                          *482-9739*
*325 North Main, near Manzanita St.*

This pretty little 1898 Victorian house is set well back from the Main Street traffic, with parking off a driveway shared with the Woods House, next door to the north. Walking to the festival from this location would be possible, but rather longer than many people would enjoy.

The Bluebell has a simple, farm house feel inside, but its small rooms are decorated with considerable style. Two bedrooms, with queen and twin size beds, are available, one upstairs with an assigned bath on the main floor, and one on the main floor, with private bath. The rates are $58 and $65, respectively.

There is air conditioning here, full breakfasts are served, and small children are accepted. Unfortunately, the Inn is only open for a short season in the summer months.

### Chanticleer Bed and Breakfast Inn                482-1919
### 120 Gresham St.

The owners of the Chanticleer, Jim and Nancy Beaver, hold seminars for would-be innkeepers and provide every imaginable special service to their own guests, from loaner umbrellas by the door to mints on the pillows. Some of their extra services are quite unusual: there are room phones and a TV is tucked away in a living room cabinet; coffee and cookies are laid out for guests to help themselves, and the refrigerator is stocked with wine and cold drinks as well; most original and welcome are play scripts and a booklet of local information in each room.

The house is a rather plain, turn-of-the-century bungalow which has been gutted and rebuilt. The result is light and fresh, but quite modern in feeling in spite of the original features that remain. There are six rooms with private baths and a large suite of two rooms, bath and kitchen that was once the owner's unit — they live next door now. All are decorated in the height of contemporary cottage style, with sprigged fabrics and dried flowers in delicate colors and country antiques. There is air conditioning, double glazing and a location quiet enough to sleep with open windows. The beds are provided with luxurious comforters and feather pillows. Only dark window coverings are missing for perfect comfort.

There are several tables used for breakfast, both in the sunny dining room and in the living room next door, so guests tend to eat separately. I was served muffins and a fruit drink made with raspberries from the garden and a single egg baked with cheese in a ramekin and accompanied by half a veal sausage with chutney and sliced melon. It was elegantly presented and exceptionally delicious, and I appreciated the small servings, though heartier appetites might not be satisfied.

The Beavers were quoted in the local paper as recommending maximum services and rates as high as the traffic will bear as keys to successful innkeeping. Rates for two of $79 in the small rooms, $89 in the rooms with two beds, and $130 in the suite certainly follow that recipe. There is a cabinet of items for sale in the front hall, with travel books, jars of jam, T-shirts with the inn's logo and bunches of dried flowers. The pictures on the living room walls are from a gallery whose price list is on the mantel. There is even a charge for local telephone calls. All this frank commercialism and the relative invisibility of the hosts — I was greeted by Mr. Beaver and thereafter saw only employees — make the Chanticleer feel more like a hotel than someone's home. But it's a very well run hotel, indeed, and the level of service is at least as high as the prices.

### The Coach House
482-2257
*70 Coolidge St., at the corner of North Main*

The Coach house is another inn that is only open for the summer season. It is located close to the street and on a very noisy corner, but the windows are double glazed and the rooms are air conditioned. This is a possible choice for non-drivers as the hosts provide airport pick-up service, though it's quite a long walk to the festival, and North Main, with its fast traffic, is not the pleasantest route.

Three rooms, each with double beds and assigned baths are rented at $49. Continental breakfast is served at the large dining room table. The hosts are young and their house has an informal coziness about it, with a normal amount of wear and tear visible. Young people who live on a budget themselves will feel right at home.

In past years the owners of the Coach House have run wine and cheese tours. They were not clear about continuing them, but should be knowledgeable guides for anyone wanting advice on touring such places on their own.

### The Country Walrus Inn
488-1134
*2785 East Main Street*

The Country Walrus is located on the other side of the freeway from the town; If you're coming off I-5 at exit #14, go past the Ashland Hills and Flagship motels and turn left at the bottom of the hill. It's just three miles to the festival from here, but it feels quite rural and isolated.

The inn is an 1886 farm house, but all trace of antiquity has disappeared from the interior. The furnishings are miscellaneous and homey and the owner's collection of dolls covers nearly every surface.

There is a sense of grandmotherly clutter, and indeed, the inn is run in casual Texas style by the mother of a former Festival actor.

Two upstairs bedrooms with queen size beds (one has an additional single) share a bath that's roomy but lacks any special B&B touches. The beds are comfortable, there is air conditioning, dark blinds cover the windows, and with the windows closed, it is quiet. Unfortunately, the sense of rural calm is marred by the sounds of highway traffic and a buzzing street light if you try for fresh air. Also unfortunate is the sulfur smell of the well water, though there is bottled water available for drinking.

The Country Walrus is one of several Ashland B&B's that are for sale. The owner is frank to say that she is burned out and wants to rejoin her son. With a new owner, the style may change, as may the rate, which is presently $55 for two. The present owner's breezy style makes for pleasant morning conversation, but her contention that not enough people like decaf to make it worth serving is symptomatic of a rather off-hand approach to the niceties of inn keeping.

*The Country Willows Inn*                                            *488-1590*
*1313 Clay Street, off Siskiyou at the south end of town*

Honking geese greet you as you drive into the yard here. You're at the end of a street of houses and yet the sense of rural peace is complete. There are even horses grazing in the field along with the ducks and geese. An unusually interesting couple has started a new life together here, in a new town and in the new business of innkeeping. Their enjoyment of it all is contagious.

This is another old farmhouse that has been totally renovated; only the previous owner's pine paneled study was left as the present owners found it. Some of the old newspapers that were found in the walls are framed and hung in the living room. The barn, in which an apartment has been built for the owners' children to stay when visiting, is quite old and worth a visit.

Four upstairs bedrooms are furnished with a variety of beds, including a king size one with a canopy that was custom made for the inn. All have private baths, air conditioning, luxurious towels and quilts and real down pillows. Nights are beautifully quiet and dark here. There is also a separate guest house which will accommodate up to four people. Rates are $75 and $85.

Very few cutesy touches mar the simple elegance of Country Willows, and the special features are real — those expensive pillows, a swimming pool — not meaningless mints on the pillow. The telephone for guests is in the study, which is nice and private, and there is a television set there, too. Breakfast, featuring french toast made from home baked bread and broiled grapefruit, was particularly good. This is one of the best B&B's anywhere.

*Cowslip's Belle Lodging*                                              488-2901
*159 North Main St., at Bush St.*

I spent a gloomy evening leaning on the kitchen door of the Cowslip's Belle while the hosts did the advance work for the next morning's breakfast and filled me in on all the local gossip. I must have slowed their preparations, but they made me feel like their personal friend, and I suspect they do that with all their guests, one way or another. If the secret of a successful inn is the innkeepers, and I think it is, it may soon be hard to get a room here on a Monday in January.

The Cowslip's Belle is housed in a handsome craftsman bungalow with lots of dark woodwork and beveled, leaded glass. Two of the guest rooms are on the main floor and two are in a remodeled carriage house at the rear of the garden. Three of the rooms have queen and single beds and private baths. The fourth is smaller, with a queen bed and an assigned bath right next door. Rates for two range from $60 to $70 ($45 to $55 in winter and on week nights in spring and fall). Special touches here include down comforters on the beds and a home made chocolate truffle on your pillow the first night of your visit (the Reinhardts make truffles for several Ashland restaurants and also sell them by mail).

The breakfast certainly didn't suffer from my distracting the cooks. That morning's menu included home-baked brioche, fresh peach pan dowdy, crustless spinach quiche and a fresh strawberry smoothie — all of it as good food as I've had anywhere.

Cowslip's Belle is a moderately easy walk to the festival. There is central air conditioning and the windows are double glazed, and perhaps because the street is level here, traffic noise is not bothersome even in the front rooms. It's hard to think of anything I'd change here.

*Edinburgh Lodge*                                                     488-1050
*686 East Main S.*

Through its transformation into a B&B and its recent sale, the J.T. Currie Boarding House has retained much of its original flavor. Some people will find it quaint and charming and others will think it's insufficiently elegant. There are two rooms on the first floor and four on the second, all with private baths. The rooms are very small and some of the walls are paneled with plywood. The furniture is old, as in thrift shop rather than antique store, and the linens are not always matched or in perfect repair. But there is an artless homeyness about everything here — it certainly feels more genuinely old than most of the fancier places. And there are also indications that the new owner will be upgrading things.

The inn is located just past the beginning of Siskiyou Blvd., right behind the Stratford Inn, with parking at the rear of the Stratford's lot, off Sherman Street. East Main is quiet here, but the highway traffic on Siskiyou can be heard in the upstairs rear rooms, just the reverse of the usual pattern, though it's not too loud. There is central air conditioning for hot nights.

One of the original owners came from Scotland and the rooms are named for castles. Afternoon tea is still served, but the breakfast had more to do with Ashland than Edinburgh. It would be fun to get baps and porridge, or a mixed grill, or perhaps even kippers, instead of the ubiquitous muffins and omelets, but the Scottish theme hasn't been carried that far as yet. Rates for two are $65 from June through September, which seems high for these rooms, and $49 during the rest of the year, which would seem a more appropriate price.

*Four-Fifty-Five B Street Bed and Breakfast Inn*      *488-1362*
*455 B St., at 4th St.*

Sleek and modern is not the typical style of B&B's; ruffles and antiques are far more often the theme. But 455 B Street, though an old house, has been remodeled and decorated in stark simplicity that would be at home in "Architectural Digest".

Only two rooms are available for guests here. They have been created by finishing in the attic and the resulting spaces have some serious drawbacks. For one thing, the ceilings are low, less than seven feet high in the center and sloped at the sides. for another, each room has only a single, narrow window centered in the long gable wall. If you are tall or claustrophobic, this isn't your place. The smaller room, with a queen bed, is $55; the larger, with a double plus a single, is $60

On the plus side, the rooms have built in sinks and closets and are attractively decorated. There are individual air conditioners, and although they are noisy, the area is quiet enough to sleep with the window open. The guest's bath is large and handsome and is equipped with supplies of towels and bath mats and a hamper "so nobody has to keep track." Since the bath is downstairs, on the main floor, those bedroom sinks are especially convenient. Other pleasant touches include cotton kimonos and fresh flowers from the garden in each room, and door locks.

Breakfast is served in the dining room and consisted of particularly nice raspberries and wonderful croissants and pastries, fresh that morning from Mana From Heaven. The hosts are very pleasant people, interesting to talk to, and their bright, funny three-year-old is a definite asset. This is one B&B where children of any age are welcome — under two they're free.

*Gresham House*                                   *482-1173*
*51 Gresham St., across from the library*

Gresham House is a turn of the century home where the upstairs has been enlarged and remodeled into guest quarters. Here there are two bedrooms with queen-sized beds (one with an extra single, too) and private baths. They share a sitting room, making an ideal arrangement for two couples travelling together. The original house was remodeled in craftsman style in 1910 and the hosts, one of whom is a carpenter, has continued in this style for the recent additions. He has even built craftsman headboards and light fixtures out of oak to keep the period look.

A glorified continental breakfast is served in the upstairs sitting room — guests live quite separately from the host family in this B&B. There is always fresh fruit and Mana From Heaven pastry, and usually something special too, such as bagels with cream cheese and salmon. The coffee is served in a thermos and there is a toaster oven available, so guests can help themselves when they feel like eating.

The rooms here are air conditioned and the street is reasonably quiet, too, though cars have to accelerate for the hill and will be noisier as a result. Children are welcome — the hosts have two of their own, aged five and seven. Gresham House is open when the Shakespeare Festival is, and it's an easy walk to the theatres. The rate for two is $78.

*The Hersey House*                                         *482-4563*
*451 North Main St., at the corner of Nursery St.*

The Hersey House has a straightforward, calm quality about it that reflects the very pleasant sisters who run it. They are friendly and natural and their inn is decorated handsomely but without fuss or pretension. This is another rather plain farm house from the turn of the century that has been totally renovated, but considerable architectural charm remains, especially in the living and dining rooms with their dark woodwork and built-ins. Four upstairs bedrooms with private baths are available for $70 midweek, $75 on weekends. Each is furnished with pieces in a particular style and decorated with one pattern that is used for bed linens, curtains and wall paper, even for lamp shades. The effect is sophisticated and uncluttered.

This is meticulous innkeeping, and there are a number of those distinguishing touches that make B&B's special. Wine, iced tea and cheese and crackers are laid out in the afternoon and sherry is available later. Chocolate kisses in a silver basket are left when the bed is turned down. There are telephone jacks in each room and a phone can be borrowed for calling in privacy. In addition to the usual collection of restaurant menus in the living room, there are a book for guests' comments on restaurants, and a binder with brochures and clippings and guests' reports on local attractions. There was some very unusual information made available this way, such as the location and height of nearby waterfalls gleaned from one of the local papers by the exceptionally thoughtful hosts.

Breakfast here was served at the big dining room table and was unusually good; one of their recipes is featured in a bed and breakfast recipe book. There is central air conditioning and double glazing, but the traffic is audible, especially in the front rooms, even with the windows closed. But that is about the only flaw in an otherwise delightfully comfortable and welcoming inn.

*Highland Acres*                                         *482-2170*
*1350 East Nevada St.*

Though only a little farther from the center of town than the freeway exit motels and Country Walrus (it's 3.4 miles from East Main and Pioneer), Highland Acres really feels remote enough to be listed with the out of town group. It's a long drive on deserted country roads, out Oak Street and under the freeway, but when you arrive you are rewarded with exceptional tranquility.

The house is quite new, probably built forty years ago and much remodeled since. It sits by itself on a landscaped square carved out of the surrounding fields. Two bedrooms in the house, with Queen and single beds and private baths, and a separate two room cottage with two beds and a kitchenette are rented to guests. The rates are $65 to $80, with no tax as the house is outside the city limits. The rooms are fairly small and are decorated with antiques and lots of patterned wallpapers and little objects. There is no air conditioning, but there is a swimming pool and a spa available to guests.

The hosts here have a bouncy dog and a baby and are both involved in local theatre work. This is the only B&B at which a host actually sat down and ate with me, and I enjoyed talking over a shared breakfast. If there is a disadvantage here, other than the distance from town, it is that the hosts don't sufficiently appreciate the blissful quiet of their location. The fountain in their goldfish pond burbles, though they will turn it off at night if asked, their clock chimes every fifteen minutes, and they play the hi-fi before breakfast.

*The Iris Inn Bed and Breakfast*          488-2286
*59 Manzanita St., off North Main St.*

The stern old couple in the picture on the stairs built a very solid, spacious house that would seem quite at home on a farm in New England or the Midwest. In Ashland it is set in an unusually large garden with vegetables and fruit trees, very rural and serene in feeling even though it is only half a block off North Main. Traffic noise is noticeable in the rooms on that side of the house, when the windows are open, but it's not very loud. The walk from here to the festival is moderately long.

Four upstairs bedrooms furnished with a mix of queen and twin beds share two modern bathrooms. A supply of guest towels and bath mats, and a hamper that started life as an ice-box, help make these baths pleasant to use. Other comfortable details include cotton kimono robes in each room, ceiling fans and central air conditioning, double glazing and door locks. Rates are $60 for two ($45 after November 1st).

Breakfast is served between 8:00 and 9:30, at two tables for four. The Lambs (no relation to the Ashland Guest Villa Lambs) made poached eggs with green tomatos from their garden, served like eggs benedict with English muffins and an herbed cheese sauce, the morning I was there. They offer cold drinks when you arrive and put decanters of wine and sherry in the living room each evening.

The Iris is a very comfortable place to stay. The furniture is mostly turn of the century oak, and while a collection of bells fills a glass fronted book shelf, there is no dust collecting clutter here. Several large, well behaved cats share the inn — notice the elegantly arched cat exit in the screen door to the back deck. That deck, looking over the garden to the hills across the valley, makes a pleasant place to sit and enjoy your afternoon glass of wine and talk with your fellow guests.

*The J.M. McCall House*                              *482-9296*
*153 Oak St., just below C St.*

Ashland pioneer John McCall built himself one gloriously ornate house in 1883. Since then it has fallen on hard times, become law offices and, for the past six years or so, it has been a bed and breakfast run by Phyllis Courtney, who acted at the festival for several years and since then has appeared with other local theatres. Currently it is for sale, so things may be quite different in the future.

There are six guest rooms in all. One, on the main floor, has a fireplace, a private bath and spectacular Victorian walnut furniture. Four more on the second floor have pleasant but newer furniture, with a variety of bed sizes, and share two baths. The sixth is a huge modern room and bath with two double beds that was added above the owner's suite, at the rear of the house. The rates are $68 for either of the rooms with private baths and $58 for the four others.

At present, the potential elegance of the house is seriously impaired by its shabby condition. The exterior paint is peeling and the interior could use redecorating, too. The location is ideal, though traffic noise is a problem and there is no air conditioning. Breakfast is served in the dining room, which is large enough to accommodate all the guests at once, at several tables. Unfortunately the eggs and bacon were cold and there was no decaf coffee. New owners can be expected to take renewed interest in both the appearance of the house and the comfort of the guests.

*The Lithia Rose*                              *482-1882*
*163 Granite St., facing Lithia Park, opposite the band shell*

It's a short walk through Lithia Park to the Festival from the Lithia Rose, but a dark one at night. It is marvelously quiet here, facing the park, and the wicker chairs on the front porch get constant use. The cozy living room, with its dark craftsman woodwork and chintz covered furniture, also was occupied more than is usual in B&B's, perhaps in part because most of the bedrooms here are small.

There are five bedrooms, with a variety of different sized beds in them, that share three baths. The rooms are stylishly decorated with a moderate amount of antique clutter, old books and chamber pots and the like, and enjoy attractive views of the neighborhood greenery. They are not air conditioned, but fortunately it's quiet enough to sleep with the windows open here. All the rooms are $65 for two.

The baths are large and have modern stall showers. The original six foot tub in the main floor bathroom looked tempting but was not in usable condition. Towels and soap are provided in the guests' rooms and no provision is made for individual mats or fingertip towels in the baths.

Breakfast was served at 9:00 in the dining room at two tables pushed together, a tight squeeze for nine or ten people, but good for conversation. The food was plentiful but not particularly distinguished. The Lithia Rose is run by a very informal, relaxed host; her style is reflected in both the very inviting public areas and in the minor lapses from spit and polish innkeeping.

### The Miners Addition                                          482-5334
*737 Siskiyou Blvd., between Alida and Morton Sts.*

The glass panel in the front door of the Miner's Addition has been etched with a picture of miners' tools, a nice touch as you begin your visit here. The house is small and simple, quite believable as a miner's boarding house, though the furnishings are a rather feminine clutter of prints and pillows in which it's hard to imagine a miner.

Two rooms are available for guests. One is large and irregularly shaped, with both a queen sized bed and a single, and a cute private bath tucked into a corner under the eves. The other is smaller, has a queen bed and a couch, and a bath that's half in the room — the toilet and basin — and half across the hall — the shower.

The rate for either of these rooms is $55 for two and includes a continental breakfast. The rooms have individual air conditioners and some traffic noise as they are close to a busy street.

### The Morical House                          482-2254
*668 North Main St.*

The Morical House is named for its present owners, who developed it into a bed and breakfast, not for its original builder. It is a sprawling, shingled house set in really handsome gardens between the highway and the railroad tracks. At first glance it looks like a craftsman bungalow, but once inside you discover its Victorian core. The little, vertical rooms are a surprise, masked on the outside by later additions.

Much of the Victorian detailing is actually modern, reproduced in the course of remodeling the house into a B&B. Five guest rooms on the second and third floors each have a private bath. There is lots of handsome antique furniture, and the decor is country Victorian without being overwhelmingly cute. The rate for two is $70.

Pleasant touches here include a telephone on a cord long enough to reach into the rooms, wine and hot hors d'oeuvres in the afternoon, and golf clubs and balls for putting on the huge lawn. There is also a bar with an electric kettle where guests can make themselves a cup of tea or get an iced drink. Breakfast is served at individual tables in the dining room and the adjacent sun porch, which overlook the gardens and the hills beyond. The table settings are exceptionally elegant, and the food was skillfully cooked and served, but there is no friendly conversation between the guests.

In addition to the lack of breakfast table fellowship, there are some serious deficiencies in the comfort of the rooms. Some people may not mind, but I found the bed to be bruisingly hard. I also was bothered by the light shining into the room, both street lights coming through the white window blinds and the hall lights coming through the glass transom over the door. Worst of all was the traffic noise and the train at the bottom of the garden; when it goes by, if you're alive, you'll wake up with a start.

### Oak Hill                          482-1554
*2190 Siskiyou Blvd., at Clay St.*

Florence Hill retired from teaching to open a bed and breakfast in an old shingled house at the south end of town. The first stage of remodeling was nearly finished when I visited and she hoped to open soon with three or four rooms. Each will have a private bath and a remote controlled television. Eventually she plans to develop a room that's accessible to handicapped visitors and a suite for families traveling with children. A patio for guests to lounge on and a garden with vegetables and berries to use for breakfast are also on the drawing board.

The living and dining rooms here are big and comfortable, and the hostess, with her energetic little terrier trotting behind, is so friendly that this should be a delightful place to stay. There isn't much traffic this far out on Siskiyou, and there is central air conditioning. Rates for two are scheduled to be $65 and include a full breakfast.

*Oak Street Station*                                                    *482-1726*
*239 Oak St., at B St.*

Oak Street Station is everybody's grandmother's house — tree shaded lawn, rocking chair on the porch, cozy rooms in old fashioned colors full of the souvenirs of a long life. That the innkeepers have created all this, more or less instantly, doesn't detract from its nostalgic charm.

Three and a half bedrooms and one elegantly appointed little bath comprise the guest quarters here. Three bedrooms have queen sized beds; the half, the former sewing room, only has room for a single. That little room is one of the pleasantest I've stayed in, but it's mostly used when someone brings a child or needs two beds. The central air conditioning is exceptionally quiet, and so is the neighborhood, so open windows are no problem. The bath is supplied with mats and guest towels and a hamper and is fastidiously clean. The cost is $60 for two, $50 for the small single.

Breakfast was served to all the guests squeezed around the dining room table. The menu was unusual but tasty: a poached fresh pear, cold ham rolled with cream cheese and hot stuffed mushrooms, and apple squares. Good conversation and friendly hosts made this a memorable visit.

*The Queen Anne*                                                    *482-0220*
*25 North Main St., just north of the plaza*

The Queen Anne, in spite of its name, is an Italianate Victorian, one of the Three Sisters that stand high above the west side of North Main. It is listed on the National Register of Historic Places and so was transformed into a bed and breakfast without changing the exterior.

Inside, the essential renovations have been handled with sensitivity and without a trace of imitation Victorian glitz. The colors are sophisticated and the original floors have been refinished, revealing the pale wood and displaying the hosts' oriental rugs to perfection. The furnishings are the fine things they have accumulated, not cute antiques, and the mineral collection is a unique addition to the decor. Don't think of little rocks in cotton lined boxes; these are serious specimens.

The upstairs guest bedrooms are as elegantly decorated as the rest of the house and have queen beds, plus an extra single bed in one, and private baths or an assigned bath on the main floor. The rates are $65 and $70. Air conditioning is being installed this year, and the windows are double glazed, so that with the house set so far above and back from the traffic, the noise is not too bad, even in the front bedroom. The light and airiness and views from high on the bluff are exceptional; the pioneers knew just where to put their houses. The worst part of walking to the

Ashland's first hospital was located on East Main, where the Columbia Hotel is now; moved around the corner, it is now the Winchester Inn. *Ashland Public Library, print by Terry Skib*

147

festival from here is coming back up the steep front steps, but you can always use the more level driveway, reached from the alley off High St.

A full breakfast is served here, with the food on platters that the guests pass around and help themselves from, family style. The conversation lasts through the leisurely meal with the retired English teacher host contributing his knowledge to discussions of the plays. The Queen Anne is closed during the winter.

### *The Romeo Inn*                            *488-0884*
### *295 Idaho St.*

The Romeo Inn is a colonial from the forties, with modern additions, and is furnished and decorated like a contemporary family home. Four huge rooms, two upstairs and two on the main floor, each have king size beds and private baths. A newly built suite over the garage features a marble fireplace, a two-person whirlpool bath, a bedroom with king size bed, a living room with vaulted ceiling, and a kitchen. The rates are $84 in the upstairs rooms, $96 and $106 in the main floor rooms, which each have an additional single bed, though there is an additional $20 charged for a third guest, and $138 for the suite.

These are about the highest prices charged in Ashland. The space and separation between rooms, the king size beds and the absolute quiet of the neighborhood are exceptional. There is a solar heated swimming pool and a spa, and a nice, secluded patio where guests can sit. You are offered afternoon tea and little chocolate hearts are left in your room at bedtime. However, breakfast, which is served over a long period so that guests tend to eat in shifts, was not spectacular, the bedroom furnishings and decoration are are not particularly luxurious, and it is a fairly long walk to the festival. It certainly is a comfortable inn, run by very pleasant, friendly hosts, but I'm not sure it is worth these prices when there are other great places to stay that cost much less.

### *RoyAl Carter House*                        *482-5623*
### *514 Siskiyou Blvd., at the corner of Union St.*

The unusual spelling of the name of this inn comes from the names of the hosts, Roy and Alyce Levy, and the original owners, the Carters. The Carters were bankers, well-off but childless according to the Levys, and so their grand house has only a few, huge bedrooms. Upstairs are two master bedroom suites each with two rooms containing four beds. The rate in these is $60 for two plus $15 for each additional person. One smaller upstairs room with a queen bed is $44. All three have private baths and central air conditioning. On the main floor the former billiard room has a king size bed, a bath with a big dressing area and french doors to the garden, but no air conditioning. The rate for it is $55. These are bargain rates for rooms of this quality, with private baths, a full breakfast and a relatively easy walk downtown.

A delicious breakfast featuring a baked cheese and tomato dish was served in the immense dining room. This is one place where a full house would not crowd the table. The Levys are involved in many aspects of Ashland civic affairs and talking to them over breakfast was an education, and a very entertaining one.

No cost was spared in building this house, and in 1909 you got a solid result for your money. Traffic noise scarcely dares penetrate. The furnishings are homey, much what a family would accumulate, with no self conscious attempt at period decor. There have been some modern changes made, including attractive decking in the garden and very inappropriate shingles in the stairwell and the upstairs hall. There is also a back yard swimming pool that unfortunately doesn't meet the code for guest use, which is a pity as it looks most inviting on a hot day.

*The Stepsister* 488-1656
*115 North Main, Opposite Bard's Inn, just beyond the plaza*
At the end of a row of glorious Victorians known locally as the Three Sisters, among them the Queen Anne, sits a craftsman bungalow. It's a handsome house, large, light and full of original woodwork and detailing, with no need to apologize, but the hosts have a nice sense of humor. In addition to the name of the inn, you can enjoy their message if you call while they're unavailable, "doing the glamor jobs of innkeeping, like plumbing repairs."

Two guest rooms are available here, each costing $64. Upstairs is the former sleeping porch with queen bed, private bath and air conditioning. On the main floor is a bedroom with original wood trim, a queen bed and a private bath but at present no air conditioning, though that may be changed according to the hosts. Both rooms face the rear garden, not the noisy street, and there is double glazing too.

A continental breakfast is served, and so is afternoon tea. Parking is in the lot next door. Unfortunately, the Stepsister is open only during the summer season. You can't get much closer to the festival than this, and it is a lovely, serene house.

*The Winchester Inn*                                                488-1113
*35 South Second St.*

In this country anywhere you stay and get breakfast is called a B&B; in England, where all beds come with breakfast, the Winchester Inn would be called a country house hotel. There are seven rooms and a full restaurant and no sense whatever of visiting in someone's home. Three of the rooms are on a lower floor and feel a bit subterranean, while the remaining four are upstairs. All are furnished with antiques and have private baths and individual air conditioners. The high season rate for two in any of the rooms is $89 ($59 in winter and $69 midweek in spring and fall), up substantially from the $72 charged in 1987.

I have been told that the ownership and management of the inn has been reorganized and I hope that the new regime improves the maintenance and service along with raising the rates. When I arrived I had to walk back to the kitchen and interrupt the conversation there to get someone to show me to my room. And the room, which wasn't the one I had asked for, had stains on the carpet, peeling paint and dripping faucets in the bath, and a strong smell of cigarette smoke plus scented air freshener. Worst of all, the kitchen ventilator throbbed from the floor below and was only turned off when, at 12:30 AM, I complained to the owner. That was the only time during my visit that I saw him in the hotel.

Staying here makes it clear that the restaurant is the focus of this inn, a fact that neither repairs nor improved service is likely to change. The dining area and kitchen take up most of the main floor. There is a tiny lounge with complimentary sherry, a telephone and a portable black and white TV for the residents, but it is also used by diners waiting for their tables. Guests do get a choice of elaborate breakfast entrees — the restaurant breakfasts and the ideally close location are The Winchester's best features.

*Wisteria House*                                                    488-2302
*435 Allison St., off Gresham St., behind the Library*

Wisteria House has a kind of cheerful, unstudied friendliness that I'm sure reflects the innkeepers' family; it closes when the host's daughter goes back to school and can't help anymore. The house is old and painted white with green trim and the inside is filled with the kind of antiques and collectables that you can imagine were accumulated through years of yard sales and weekend antiquing trips. And yes, the front porch is covered with wisteria.

Three upstairs bedrooms with double beds and air conditioning are rented to guests. One, with a private bath, is $45 for two. The two others, which share a bath, are rented as a suite for $65 for two. These are among the lowest rates available. In keeping with the casual style here, the coffee pot is always on and breakfast is served in the kitchen or out on the deck: fresh fruit and juice and breakfast breads with locally made jam and jelly.

It's quite convenient walk from here to the festival or the plaza area — about three or four long blocks along either Hargadine or East Main. The alley to the parking area is off Gresham St.; latecomers to the plays have to park almost this far away every day, so why not enjoy the walk?

*The Woods House*                                                                  *488-1598*
*333 North Main St.*

Dr. and Mrs. Woods built this craftsman bungalow in 1908 and raised a family of four sons there. It has been extensively modernized but still retains its warmth. The furnishings are an eclectic mixture of old and new and the decor is only a little bit cluttered — it may be impossible to buck the trend in such a trendy business.

There are six guest rooms, each with its own bath and a variety of beds, from double to king. Two are on the main floor, two are upstairs and two more are in the carriage house. Rooms with one bed cost $55 for a small one in the carriage house with a double or $60 for the ones on the main floor of the house, which have queens. The rest have two beds and go for $70. There is parking behind the carriage house and a pleasant garden, but no air conditioning. On a hot night with the windows open, the Main Street traffic would be pretty loud.

When the inn is full as many as eighteen people sit down to breakfast in the dining room, requiring two sittings. The innkeeper's background in hotel management has helped her organize the smooth running of this big operation. Coffee and cookies are always available and guests are offered breakfast choices with unusual consideration for special diets and health requirements. The Woods House is among the inns that are for sale because the innkeeper wants to rejoin her husband who works in

California. I hope the new owner will possess the same combination of warmth and competence.

Because there are relatively few rooms available in B&B's in Ashland, I have given brief descriptions of some in other areas nearby for those who cannot find what they want in town. The geographical cut off is arbitrary; some I have reviewed in detail are in fact slightly outside of the city limits and some of these have Ashland addresses. I have not stayed at these out of town inns.

Near the South Ashland exit #11 from I-5:

*Neil Creek House*                                                    *482-1334*
*341 Mowetza*

Two rooms with private baths, air conditioning and full breakfast with hosts who have come to Ashland from Germany (they can provide Shakespeare texts in German as well as English and "Scrabble with Umlauts"). Rates are $75 ($65 when the festival is closed) with a three day minimum stay. The owners had their inn on the market but have now decided to stay and limit their hospitality to returning guests and their friends.

*Shutes Lazy S Farm*                                                    *482-5498*
*200 Mowetza*

The Shutes run a real farm and rent one room with a double bed, private bath and air conditioning, for $55. Breakfast features home grown food and they prefer guests to stay a minimum of two days in order to get to know them.

Near the Mt. Ashland exit from I-5:

*Mt. Ashland Inn*                                                    *482-8707*
*550 Mt. Ashland Rd.*

Bed and breakfast in a log house that has four rooms with private baths; rates are $60 to $70 with breakfast. There is no air conditioning, but at 5500 feet up on a mountain, perhaps it isn't needed.

*Treon's Country Homestay*                                                    *482-0746*
*1819 Colestin Rd.*

Visitors who take a Backstage Tour get to see how the Elizabethan Stage feels to the performers. *Oregon Shakespearean Festival, photo Hank Kanziev*

This rustic 2 bedroom bed and breakfast with a shared bath costs $50 for two; they are part of the B&B reservation network and are the only one permitting smoking. Ski packages are available.

In Medford:

> *Under the Greenwood Tree*                                776-0000
> *3045 Bellinger Lane, Medford, about two miles from Jacksonville*
> Four rooms, two with sitting rooms, all with private baths, on a mid-

153

nineteenth century farm — they'll give you a tour of the old buildings. High season rates for two are from $65 to $75 and include high tea, sherry, chocolate truffles on your pillow and a full breakfast.

In Jacksonville:

*The Farm House*                                                        *899-8963*
*755 East California St.*

A three bedroom, 1929 Dutch Colonial with private baths and air conditioning. In the summer, when they are open, the rate is $55.

*Jacksonville Inn*                                                      *899-1900*
*175 East California St.*

This is a much renovated Gold Rush era inn with eight rooms. Antique furnishings and exposed brick walls combine happily with modern private baths and air conditioning. The rate is $50, including breakfast in the dining room with a choice of entrees.

*Livingston Mansion*                                                   *899-7107*
*4132 Livingston Rd.*

The Livingston Mansion offers three rooms with private baths and a swimming pool. They are located a mile from Jacksonville and the rate for two is $80.

*McCully House Inn*                                                    *899-1942*
*240 East California St.*

This 1861 Classical Revival house in the center of Jacksonville is on National Register; four rooms with private baths are available at $65 - $70 and credit cards are accepted.

*Reames House*                                                         *899-1868*
*540 E. California*

Accommodation for six people in an 1868 National Register Victorian within walking distance of the Britt Festival; $55 for two with full breakfast.

*Tou Velle House*                                                      *899-8938*
*455 N. Oregon*

Three guest rooms in a craftsman home with a swimming pool but no private baths. The rooms have a king, a queen or two double beds and cost $65 for two, with continental breakfast

# *Short Term Rentals*

The houses, apartments and cottages in this section are listed together because they seem to meet a need. What they have in common is kitchens, some pretty sketchy and some quite completely equipped. In a couple of cases the makings of a continental breakfast are delivered each morning, and they could have been listed as bed and breakfast inns, as their owners consider them. However, the feeling is different in a separate cottage or apartment, where you don't gather for breakfast or share the hosts' house, and that is why they are included here. All are fully furnished and daily maid service is provided.

The rates at these places are harder to compare because the number of people each will accommodate varies so widely, but here is the list:

| RENTAL RATES — IN ASHLAND | | |
|---|---|---|
| The Stone House | 1 - 2 guests | $ 30 - 40 |
| Parkside Cottage | 2 - 6 | 48 - 78 |
| Auburn Street Cottage | 2 - 4 | 66 - 86 |
| Palm Motel Houses | 4 - 8 | 70 - 96 |
| Ashland Motel House | 6 - ? | 85 |
| Enders House | 2 - 6 | 85 - 115 |
| Spiridon House | 2 - 7 | 95 - 200 |
| Colony Inn | 1 - 8 | 100 |
| B Street House | 4 - 8 | 100 - 140 |

| ...AND OUTSIDE ASHLAND | | |
|---|---|---|
| McKee Bridge Cottage | 2 - 4 | $ 50 |
| Waverly Cottage | 2 - 4 | 55 - 75 |
| Greensprings Box R Ranch | 10 - 16 | 60 - 80 |
| Soaring Hawks | 1 - 6 | 125 - 150 |
| Mathew's Inn | 2-7 | 150 |

Motel units with kitchens can give you some of this same sense of independence. They range from standard bedrooms with closet kitchenettes to sizable apartments. The Ashland Motel, the Cedarwood, the Flagship Quality Inn, the Hillside Inn, Jackson Hot Springs, the Manor Motel, the Palm Motel, the Stratford Inn, and the Timbers Motel all offer units with some sort of kitchen facilities.

A few bed and breakfast inns also have suites with kitchens that give you a choice of joining the inn guests for breakfast or being independent: Chanticleer, Country Willows, Highland Acres and the Romeo Inn.

### *Ashland Motel House* 482-2561
### *1145 Siskiyou Blvd.*

The Ashland Motel rents a house located around the corner on Garfield St.. It has two bedrooms, one with a king size bed and one with two singles, a large living room with a sofa bed, and there are also several roll-aways. The charge is $85 for any number of people, so with a few sleeping bags a group can live really cheaply here.

This isn't glamorous lodging, but the beds are reasonably comfortable and the kitchen is adequate for basic cooking. There is a television set and also an air conditioning unit in the dining area. The worst thing about this house is that the windows are coated with heat reflective film which makes you feel like you've forgotten to take your dark glasses off.

### *Auburn Street Cottage* 482-3004
### *549 Auburn St., off Gresham St., three blocks above East Main*

The architects who live in the main house built this charming back yard cottage to reflect its craftsman style. One large room with an open, gabled ceiling is divided into sleeping, cooking and eating spaces. The central living area has an upholstered window-seat overlooking the garden. Sleeping alcoves on either side contain double and single beds

156

with openable skylights above them. There is also a skylight in the bathroom. The kitchen is tiny but complete except that the only oven is a microwave.

The owners claim that the cottage can accommodate four people with one sleeping on the window seat and charge $66 for two plus $10 for each additional person. This isn't a big space and much of its attractiveness seems to me to lie in the serene good looks of the main area. As the single bed is also not full size, one or two adults and one child seems to me to be the maximum comfortable number of guests.

The Auburn Street Cottage is well insulated and has good ventilation but it lacks air conditioning for real comfort in the hottest weather. It is also a fairly long walk to the festival area, and a hilly one returning. Strong on the plus side, however, are the total quiet and privacy of its garden setting and the pleasure of sitting on the deck under the apple tree and looking off at the mountains.

### *The B Street House*                    482-4217
*111 B St., at Pioneer*

The Festival, the plaza and most of the downtown are within a very short walk of this house, and that's its major attraction. It is a restored 1905 bungalow with three bedrooms, one with a king, one with a queen and one with twin beds. There is also a queen size sofa bed in the living room so that up to eight guests can stay here.

This is not the funky, student rental sort of house that the motels on Siskiyou own. It is nicely painted and furnished and has a reasonably well equipped kitchen and one and a half baths. The house is close to the street, but it is not a very busy corner, so noise should not be a problem, and there is an air conditioner. The back yard is fenced and has a patio and barbecue.

The rates, which include the 6% tax, are $100 for four plus $10 for each additional person. With separate sleeping areas and the extra half bath, this house should provide comfortable accommodation for several couples traveling together at a very reasonable per couple cost.

### *Colony Inn*                    482-2668
*725 Terra Ave. at Siskiyou*

The Colony Inn is a big apartment complex at the south end of town. Each unit consists of four bedrooms with twin beds, a kitchen and a bath.

In winter the individual bedrooms are rented by the month with shared use of the kitchen and bath. In summer, whole units are rented to groups of up to eight people for $100 a night.

This is a pretty scruffy place, and people who've stayed here have confirmed my impression that it's not overly clean. However, $12.50 per person per night is a reasonable price for a group if one of the less expensive houses is not available.

### *Enders House*                                                   *482-9473*
*31 S. Second St. at Enders Alley*

Two apartments in an 1896 Queen Anne are rented to visitors. The house is next to the Winchester Inn and very convenient to the festival. The lower unit is essentially in its original form, with old fashioned woodwork and paneling. There are two bedrooms with queen beds plus a sofa bed in the living room to accommodate up to six people. There is a dining room with French doors and a fully equipped kitchen. This unit rents from $95 for two people, up to $115 for six.

The upstairs apartment has one bedroom with a queen bed plus a sofa-bed in the living room, for up to four people, and costs $85 to $95. There is a fully equipped country-style kitchen and a balcony off the living room. Both units have color cable TV and share the veranda and rear patio.

### *Palm Motel Houses*                                              *482-2636*
*1065 Siskiyou Blvd., across from SOSC*

The Palm Motel has five houses. Four are located on the quiet side street (Garfield) and are rented to college students during the school year. During the summer they are available for $70 for four people, plus $6 for each additional person. Each house has two or three bedrooms and an assortment of different sized beds and hide-a-bed sofas to sleep up to eight people. Each also has one air conditioner, a color television, and telephone jacks, in case you plan to stay long enough to make the installation cost worthwhile. The kitchens are equipped only for basic cooking and the furniture is comfortable if a bit funky. There are private lawn and picnic areas behind each of them.

The most recently acquired house is next to the motel office on Siskiyou and is currently being readied for year round rental at $85. There are two bedrooms with queen beds plus a porch off the dining room with a sofa bed. Both the decoration and the furniture are much nicer than in the Garfield St. houses and a second bath is planned. However, this house faces the heavy Siskiyou traffic and is noisier than the others.

These houses are excellent value for families; the motel pool and its big lawn areas are good for soaking up children's energy, and having separate rooms does a lot for parents' morale.

### Parkside Cottage                                           482-2320
*171 Granite St., across from Lithia Park*

Parkside Cottage advertises as a bed and breakfast, but both units have kitchens and the breakfast is minimal ingredients, which the hosts leave for you in the refrigerator. The location is close to the Festival, through the park, and outstandingly quiet. Neither unit is air conditioned.

The cottage is separate from the house, though not far away or isolated at all. It is about the size of a garage and contains a queen size bed, a full kitchen and a small bath. It is suitable for only two people and rents for $48.

The suite occupies the ground floor of the main house (you can hear the family upstairs) and consists of two bedrooms, one with a queen bed and the other with a double and a single, a living room with a studio couch, a dining table and a portable TV, a minimal kitchenette and the original bathroom. Across the front, facing the park, is a covered porch that invites sitting outside. The rate here is $68 for four plus $5 per additional person.

In the winter, and on weekdays in spring and fall, the rates here are cut dramatically, the cottage to $25 and the suite to $30 for two people using only the front bedroom or $38 for four.

### Spiridon House                                             488-1362
*353 Hargadine St., near Gresham St.*

Spiridon house is owned by the hosts of the 455 B Street Bed and Breakfast. They named their house after the Greek postman who won the first modern Olympic marathon in 1896. He was a simple man and when the king offered him a reward he asked only for a horse and cart. The hosts say they chose the name because the Ashland countryside promotes appreciation for a modest lifestyle. The choice seems a little ironic to me, given that the house is the shortest possible distance from the Festival and neither the rates nor the hosts' style of innkeeping is modest.

The house was being repainted when I saw it, but judging from 455 B Street, it will be sleek and sophisticated. The same delicious breakfast that is served on B Street is delivered to the guests on Hargadine. There are three bedrooms, sleeping up to seven people, and two baths, and the rates range from $95 for two, to $140 for four, to $200 for seven. There are fans but no air conditioning.

Hargadine turns downhill quite steeply where Spiridon house is located and the views from many of the windows and from the deck should be spectacular. Except for traffic leaving the theatres, this is not a busy street so noise should not be too great a problem. In winter, the rates are reduced and special ski packages, including transportation and lift tickets, are offered.

### The Stone House                                        482-9233
*80 Hargadine St., across the street from the Elizabethan Theatre*

Now this is really an easy walk! In fact it is close enough that you can hear the audience applaud the outdoor performances. The traffic will be heavy for a short time after the plays, but otherwise it should be quiet enough to keep the windows open — there is no air conditioning. The house itself is handsome and is listed on the National Register of Historic Places, but the rental units are a separate cottage and a basement apartment.

The cottage is tiny, possibly a model T garage that modern cars outgrew. The bed forms a loft that you reach by ladder, while underneath is a compact sitting area with a color TV, a minuscule kitchenette and a bath. The cost is $30, a bargain for this location and ideal for young people without a car.

The suite is a one bedroom apartment on the ground floor of the house. Because the first floor extends out beyond its windows and there is also a big tree, these rooms may be rather dark for some tastes. There is a king size bed and color television here, a full kitchen and a bath with a tub. The cost for it is $40.

AND A FEW MORE RENTALS OUTSIDE OF ASHLAND:

*Greensprings Box R Ranch*                                    482-1873
*16799 Highway 66*

Four modern log houses are available on this working ranch twenty-three miles east of Ashland. They have two or three bedrooms plus lofts for sleeping bags, fully equipped kitchens, laundry machines and carpeted living rooms with rock fireplaces. One is adjacent to the landing strip for fly-in guests. The houses accommodate from ten to sixteen guests each and rates are $60 and $80 per night, or $350 and $450 per week.

*Mathew's Inn*                                               482-8712
*11300 Mt. Ashland Rd.*

This is a three bedroom, two bath house ten miles from Ashland and eight from the ski area. It is set up to accommodate seven people and rents for $150 per night.

*McKee Bridge Cottage*                              899-1101, 899-8347
*On Upper Applegate Road, out of Ruch*

A fully equipped two bedroom house next to the historic covered bridge in Upper Applegate. The yard is fenced and there is laundry equipment; children and pets are welcome. The rate is $50, with week and weekend rates available.

*Soaring Hawks*                                              482-8707
*500 Mt. Ashland Rd.*

This is a hand built, contemporary octagonal house for up to three couples, located near the Mt. Ashland exit from I-5 and the ski area. The minimum 3 day stay is $375 for 1 or 2 people, $450 for 3 or more.

*Waverly Cottage &*
*Miracle Block House*                              779-4716, 776-0081
*305 N. Grape, at Fourth, Medford*

One of only two bed and breakfast inns in Medford, this consists of a two bedroom, 1898 Victorian cottage on the National Register and a one bedroom apartment in a 1923 house built of Miracle Block. There are kitchens as well as a delivered breakfast, laundry facilities, color TV, telephone and air conditioning. Rates are $55 in the Miracle Block House apartment and $65 to $75 in Waverly Cottage.

161

# *Youth Hostels and Campgrounds*

The following listings of alternative lodgings include the Ashland Hostel plus a number of campgrounds and RV parks, all but one of them outside Ashland. Some of the rentals described in the previous section are also reasonable if enough people share the cost. Individual housing is not available in SOSC dormitories. Only bonafide educational groups can be housed on campus since a suit was filed by some local motel and restaurant owners charging the College with unfair competition.

The range of costs is as follows:

| INEXPENSIVE LODGING IN AND NEAR ASHLAND | | |
|---|---|---|
| Ashland Hostel | | $ 6 - 8.50 per person |
| **CAMPING** | **Tent** | **RV Hookups** |
| Forest Service/ | | |
| BLM campgrounds | $ 0 - 4 | $ |
| Jackson Hot Springs | 4 | 7.50 - ? |
| Valley of the Rogue State Park | 7 | 11 |
| Oregon RV Roundup | 9 | 14 |
| Glenyan KOA | 12 | 15 |
| Holiday RV Park | | 13 - 15 |
| Long term RV parks | | 8 - ? |

## In Ashland

*The Ashland Hostel*                                           *482-9217*
*150 North Main St.*

A young Englishman, Ian Hyndman, owns and manages Ashland's only hostel. It is associated with both American Youth Hostels and the International Youth Hostel Federation. Membership in one of these organizations is required but can be bought for one night at a time when you arrive. And don't stop reading because you're not a youth; people of all ages enjoy the hostel experience which has become particularly popular among seniors who like to meet young people.

The location of the Ashland Hostel is first class, next door to the Main Street Inn and a short walk from the festival and the plaza shops and restaurants. Hostels are aimed at carless travelers, and though there are five parking spaces behind the house, reached from the alley off Bush St., preference for accommodation is given to travelers who come on foot or by bus or bicycle.

The hostel building is a big turn of the century bungalow. Inside are a sitting room, dining room and kitchen on the main floor. The furniture is comfortable and beat up, typical college student stuff, and the kitchen is equipped with the essentials for preparing a quick meal, not a Julia Child production. The sleeping areas are filled with double-decker metal bunks with mattresses and pillows. The rooms upstairs are for women and those on the ground floor are for men, and there are separate bathrooms, too. There are also two small rooms that can be occupied by couples or families if the hostel is not too crowded. The total capacity is thirty-five people.

The rates are $6 per person for members or $8.50 with a one night membership pass. If you don't have bedding and linen with you, sleepsacks and towels can be rented for fifty cents each. These rates are possible because guests take care of their own needs and contribute some time to the morning chores before leaving. The hostel opens at 5 PM every day, but advance reservations are accepted with a deposit of one night's fee. The showers and kitchen are available to people not spending the night. Smoking is permitted outside only, and alcohol and drugs are entirely prohibited.

Hostelling does provide cheap lodging but the point is the people from all over the world that you meet and the cooperative lifestyle. You have to dispense with elegance cheerfully and enjoy communal living for it to work for you.

The auto camp in Lithia Park. *Southern Oregon Historical Society*

*Siskiyou Trailer Village*                                    *482-1776*
*2799 Siskiyou Blvd., near I-5 exit #11*
This is the one trailer/RV park in Ashland that will take temporary tenants if space is available. It is at the southern edge of town and looks pleasantly tree shaded.

## OUT OF TOWN

Jackson County operates a series of parks and recreation areas, some of which have camp grounds. The nearest is at Emigrant Lake, five miles southeast of Ashland on Highway 66. For more information or group reservations contact:

*Parks and Recreation Department*                            *776-7001*
*Jackson County Court House, Medford, OR 97501*

The nearest state park with camping facilities is:
*Valley of the Rogue State Park*
*Off I5 between Medford and Grant's Pass*
There are facilities for trailers and RV's and spaces for tents. Rates range from $7 to $11 a night; no reservations are taken. This would be a long commute in to the festival.

The Forest Service and the Bureau of Land Management maintain both developed campgrounds and relatively primitive sites with few amenities; camping outside of designated campgrounds is also permitted in some areas. Small fees are charged for some of these sites, but none can be reserved. For information contact:

*Rogue River National Forest*      482-3333
*Ashland Ranger District*
*2200 Highway 66*

*Klamath National Forest*      916-842-3516
*1312 Fairlane Rd., Yreka*

*Bureau of Land Management*      776-4174
*3040 Biddle Rd., Medford*

Nearby commercial camping sites are:
*Glenyan KOA*      482-4138
*5310 Highway 66, Ashland*
A commercial camp with restrooms, showers, laundry facilities, store, playground and swimming pool, it is located just south of town, near Emigrant Lake. There are spaces for tents, trailers and RV's. Rates for two range from $12 with a tent to $15 for a full RV hookup. They recommend advance reservations.

*Holiday RV Park*      535-2183
*201 Fern Valley Rd., Phoenix (I5 exit 24)*      1-800-452-7970
Trailer and RV spaces in an exceptionally tidy, new park that caters to overnighters. Swimming pool, some cable TV hookups. $13 - $15 per night.

*Jackson Hot Springs*      482-3776
*2253 Highway 99, Talent*
Tent camping on a large, tree shaded lawn with picnic tables, $4. Trailer and RV spaces also available, from $7.50 up depending on

hookups and number of people. Swimming pool with mineral water, private mineral baths and massages available.

*Oregon RV Roundup*                             *535-6632*
*405 W. Valley View Rd., Talent*

Tent camping, $9, and full hookup RV spaces, $14, in an attractively green and shaded park near the freeway exit.

Highway 99 between Ashland and Medford is RV and mobile home country, with sales, storage and service facilities as well as numerous trailer parks, some of which take overnighters when space is available. Rates typically start at $8 a night. Among the nicer looking places are Royal Oaks Mobil Manor and Rogue Valley Mobile Village, both on the right as you go north.

# *Where to Eat*

Over the years, I've eaten with my family at many of the places discussed in these restaurant listings, starting with dinner at Omar's in 1952. Other places were new to me when I started this project, among them some delightful discoveries. But I've tried to have at least one meal at every place in Ashland, and at as many interesting outlying restaurants as I could. I've also tried to return to places where my first meal was particularly disappointing in order not to be too harsh on those who may just have had one off night.

On the whole I have not reviewed individual meals in the listings. Occasionally describing an unusually good dish seems the best way to characterize the place where I ate it, and sometimes a meal seems so silly that I want to share a good giggle, but I've tried to resist temptation. Menus and chefs can change rapidly, and unsuccessful dishes disappear because they prove unpopular, so such reviews would be useless in a few months at most. But I can't resist giving you my favorite example of misdirected culinary creativity as it appeared on an Ashland menu: "Caribbean Shrimp Fritters — shrimp and sharp cheddar cheese in yam and potato fritters, served with fresh salsa." That's one menu that can't change soon enough; the fritters didn't taste any better than they sound.

I have tried to give some sense of the kind of food and ambiance you'll find at each restaurant, along with an estimate of its prices and overall quality. I haven't rated them an any kind of point system — so many stars for food and so many for service. Instead, I have noted those restaurants that I feel are outstanding and have also been explicit about the problems I found. My taste is not yours — you may drool at the thought of shrimp with yams and cheddar — but my experiences should be informative.

In the listings that follow, places that serve the same kind of food are grouped together so that you can pick the one whose particular location, style or price range suits your needs. But first, some general information and comments that apply to all categories:

**Surviving Restaurant Meals** — Ashland can be fattening. It's too easy to spend your days lingering over delicious meals and sitting in theaters. There has to be a way to enjoy Ashland's charm without taking so much of it home on your hips. One solution is to get outdoors and do something active. Applauding a play, however wild your enthusiasm, just isn't aerobic. The other, of course, is to eat fewer, smaller, lighter meals.

Places that serve lighter food, or where you can order a la carte, are grouped together in the listings that follow. There are also listings for food stores; nothing you fix in a motel kitchenette or take on a picnic is likely to be as rich as either a Big Mac or a French dinner. Or you can try eating two meals instead of three. It really works well with the Festival schedule if you want to see the Green Show. You can enjoy a generous brunch without guilt and a good dinner eaten early, and as a bonus, stay awake through Shakespeare's talkiest history since you'll be all through digesting.

**Vegetarian Dining** — Everyone who's ever tried to follow a vegetarian diet knows how tiresome it is to eat in restaurants and always have to take the one meatless entree; a person can eat only so many plates of steamed vegetables with cheese. Ashland must have a sizeable population of resident vegetarians for so many restaurants to cater to them so generously. Places with more than a token meatless entree are:

*Ashland Bakery — Meatless burgers, tofu scrambles, vegie stir-fries*

*Cesar's — Meatless Mexican dishes*

*Gamekeeper's — Mixed vegetable sautes and spanakopita*

*Gepetto's — Stuffed baked potatoes, pasta and vegetarian entrees*

*Greenleaf Deli — Substantial meatless hot dishes, salads, sandwiches*

*Munchies — Bean and cheese Mexican dishes*

*North Light — Totally vegetarian restaurant serving all three meals*

*Tommy's — Vegetable quiche, lasagna, meatless Mexican dishes*

**Prices** — Eating in Ashland seems downright cheap to anyone who lives near a big, expensive city. The most extravagant dinner in town when I started this project was filet mignon of moose at $23.98, but that restaurant went out of business (without my tasting moose, thank you). In case your perspective is from an even smaller and less expensive town than Ashland, rather than from, say, San Francisco, I've categorized Ashland prices as follows:

|  | Low | Moderate | Expensive |
| --- | --- | --- | --- |
| Breakfast and lunch | under $3 | $3 to $5 | |
| Sunday brunch | | $5 to $7 | $7 to $9 |
| Dinner | under $7 | $7 to $12 | $12 to $20 |

These are the entree prices, and the cost of a meal can certainly be higher if you add lots of extras, drinks and so forth. The price of a Sunday brunch usually includes the entire meal, and most dinners include soup or salad. The bulk of a restaurant's prices are what determine its category;

The Depot Hotel Dining Room circa 1900. *Southern Oregon Historical Society*

a basically moderate place may serve a cheap vegetable plate, or surf and turf at the other extreme.

**Hours** — In summer most Ashland businesses that depend on tourists, and all the eating places do, stay open seven days a week. If they want a closed day, it's likely to be Monday, when the theatres are dark. Come fall, when the outdoor productions have closed and the tourists are fewer, the opening times and days change, and when the Festival closes down for the winter, they change again, only to go back to something like the fall schedule in spring. I hope it's clear why I have not included the days and times places are open in most of the listings; instead I've given phone numbers so you can check. I have tried to note when a restaurant is open unusually early or late, or departs from the usual Ashland pattern.

**Walking to the Plays** — Most of the restaurants are somewhere in the small area of downtown Ashland, within an easy walk of everything else, including the theatres. Places noted as near the I-5 interchange or the college are not downtown, and you can't reasonably expect to walk between them and the festival.

**Handicapped Access** — Most restaurants are level in off the street. When a place is up or down stairs from the street I have mentioned it in the listings. In some cases there is still access off an alley, so it may be worth telephoning if you need to get in with a wheelchair.

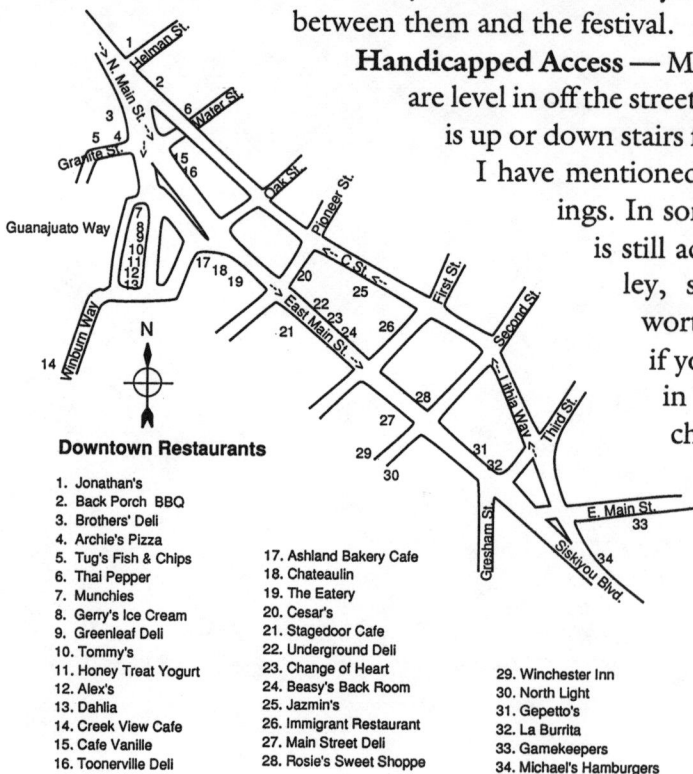

**Downtown Restaurants**

1. Jonathan's
2. Back Porch BBQ
3. Brothers' Deli
4. Archie's Pizza
5. Tug's Fish & Chips
6. Thai Pepper
7. Munchies
8. Gerry's Ice Cream
9. Greenleaf Deli
10. Tommy's
11. Honey Treat Yogurt
12. Alex's
13. Dahlia
14. Creek View Cafe
15. Cafe Vanille
16. Toonerville Deli

17. Ashland Bakery Cafe
18. Chateaulin
19. The Eatery
20. Cesar's
21. Stagedoor Cafe
22. Underground Deli
23. Change of Heart
24. Beasy's Back Room
25. Jazmin's
26. Immigrant Restaurant
27. Main Street Deli
28. Rosie's Sweet Shoppe

29. Winchester Inn
30. North Light
31. Gepetto's
32. La Burrita
33. Gamekeepers
34. Michael's Hamburgers

# *Fast Food*

Ashland has done a pretty complete job of exiling the classic fast food franchises to the other side of the tracks, literally. McDonald's, Taco Bell and Pizza Hut are all on Highway 66 between the railway overpass and the freeway interchange.

The point of these places is their predictability. A Big Mac is supposed to taste the same in Hong Kong or Paris as it does in Oregon or Texas. I haven't eaten one in any of these places and I'm willing to leave it that way, but if you get an undeniable Mac Attack your fix is available.

## PIZZA

Pizza is Ashland's staple food, to judge by the number of places that sell it. In order to reach some conclusions about the different pizzas available in Ashland I spent an afternoon buying one from each place. I tasted each one as soon as I got it, and when I had them all I went to a remote picnic table in Lithia Park and compared them. My observations follow; the price quoted is for a medium pizza with everything on it.

*Angelo's Pizza*　　　　　　　　　　　　　　　　482-8081
*1585 Siskiyou Blvd.*

Angelo's is part of a small chain (nine places, from Eureka to Medford) that is aimed at the low price market. It is an unattractive, windowless space, decorated in brown and located just beyond the college. A medium pizza is $8.70 and they offer all you can eat lunches of already cooked pizza slices and salad from the bar for $3.50 and senior citizen suppers of a small pizza with salads and drinks for two for $5.85.

Unfortunately the pizza is nearly tasteless, made with very small quantities of the toppings on a thin, crisp crust that is the best part.

### Archie's Pizza             482-2989
### 75 North Main St.

A big, battered but cheerful place downtown, Archie's is host to weekend Beatles sing-alongs that are immensely popular with local children. Some kooky flavors (Mexican, Hawaiian) are offered along with the traditional ones and they have a small salad bar, a few desserts and the usual beer, wine and soft drinks. Flavorful, thick crust, rolled to order, tasty sauce and real, stringy cheese made this the best of the seven pizzas tested, but it's still just pizza parlor style, with no gourmet aspirations. $11.15 for a loaded, twelve inch pizza; $1 for delivery.

### Domino's Pizza             488-1221
### 346 East Main St

As their ads say, Domino's delivers, or you can take it away yourself, but there is no seating here. $9.75 gets you an acceptable if not thrilling pizza, rolled out and cooked to order. The crust was fairly good, the toppings fresh and the sauce nice but a bit bland. They have promotional specials which can cut the cost significantly.

### Giseppi's New York Style Pizza       482-5559
### 1469 Siskiyou Blvd. in the Buy-Rite Shopping Center

Sad to say, the nice young man who runs Giseppi's knows just as much about pizza as he does about Italian spelling. He loaded raw vegetables onto a precooked pizza and heated them. The result was hot but raw toppings that fell off a tough and tasteless cheese-and-crust bottom. They only offer slices and large pizzas, which cost about $13.

### Gramalot Pizzeria             488-1132
### 1602 Hwy 66

This is a small restaurant next to the The Beanery, the college coffee hangout. They open for dinner only and offer free delivery. The menu lists all the typical flavors, a dinner salad and the usual drinks. A twelve inch combination pizza is $6.95. The owner rolled out the crust and made the pizza while I watched, chatting all the while. He used lots of cheese and canned, rather than fresh, toppings but very little sauce. The result was extremely soupy and tended to run off the crust as you tried to pick it up. It wasn't terribly tasty either.

*Papa D's*                                                    *482-1986*
*1448 Highway 66*

Papa D's has a more extensive menu than the other pizza places and an attractive dining room decorated with blowups of historic photographs. They serve a variety of sandwiches, burgers, hot dogs, soup and pasta as well as the usual salad bar and beverages. The poorboy sandwich I tried here was totally tasteless, an impossible achievement with that many ingredients, you would think. Their pizza, which costs $9.95 for a thirteen inch combo, was much better, a close second to Archie's, though the crust was thick and dull. Delivery is free after 5 PM, but taking it out yourself costs twenty five cents for the box!

*Pizza Hut*                                                   *488-1581*
*2205 Highway 66*

The inside of the Pizza Hut is a lot more attractive than the exterior, with big windows and comfortable booths and a salad bar in the center. At lunch they offer individual pizzas that are ready in five minutes. Mine was loaded with sauce and toppings and the thick crust was crisp and fresh tasting, with a soft interior. The flavor was somewhat artificial, with a peppery aftertaste, and I worry about what "beef topping" contains that they can't call it ground beef. A medium sized Super Supreme is $10.50.

To summarize: Archie's, Papa D's and Domino's pizzas are fairly good; Pizza Hut's, Gramalot's and Angelo's are edible; Giseppi's is hopeless.

## Hamburgers

You can get burgers, sometimes quite good ones, in coffee shops and restaurants, especially steak houses. The restaurants that follow specialize in burgers, though they have other things available too.

*Big Al's Drive-In*                                           *482-4310*
*474 North Main St.*

The hot air balloon decorations are no accident; this is where you get Big Al's Balloon Flights, too. It's more of a family restaurant than you might expect from outside, light and attractive and serving good sandwiches and salad from a bar as well as hamburgers. They also close early in the evening. However, the burgers are standard, drive-in quality, and there is the drive-in's typical deep-fried ambiance, too. Burger prices range from $1.45 to $2.65.

*The Bushes Hard Rock Burger Bar*    *482-3853*
*1474 Siskiyou Blvd.*

A drive-in for the young, open till 3 AM every night, with music videos. A huge range of burgers is offered, from a 69 cent mini to an $11, two pound monster that they have a snapshot of two football players eating. I tried something in between, but it didn't have much flavor.

*Creek View Cafe*    *482-1461*
*85 Winburn Way, across from Lithia Park*

An exceptionally clean and pleasant version of the standard resort snack bar, the cafe is open during the summer season only. There are lots of shaded tables and an air conditioned seating area, too, but no table service. They post a sign claiming that they are health oriented and use only the purest ingredients. Burgers — mine cost $3.25 and was quite tasty— and soft ice cream are the specialties. They also sell stale bread for feeding the ducks.

*Goodtimes Family Food and Fun*    *482-4424*
*1951 Highway 66*

The hamburgers, costing from $1.90 to $3.25, are only fair here. The real reason for coming is the video games and pool tables. It's a great place to park your kids while you do something more to adult taste.

*McDonald's of Ashland*    *488-2455*
*2235 Highway 66*

Just like every other McDonald's.

*Michael's Fine Hamburgers*    *482-9205*
*457 Siskiyou Blvd.*

Michael's serves big, goopy burgers from $2.75 to $4.50, depending on the extras you order. They taste quite good. They offer a few sandwiches, drinks and french fries, too. The seating area is woodsy and attractive, with music videos not played too loud, and there are tables on the patio as well.

Burger summary: None of these places makes a really superior hamburger, with lean, tasty meat and a roll with enough substance not to dissolve in the juice. Michael's came closest, and Creekview's burgers are also fairly good, but both tend to to be greasy. I've only tried the hamburgers at a few of the other Ashland restaurants, and perfection has eluded me. The best, so far, was at the Copper Skillet.

## FISH AND CHIPS

*Tug's Fish and Chips*                                    *482-5564*
*5 Granite St., just north of the plaza*

This is a pleasant, light place, behind Archie's Pizza — they share the parking lot — with tables both inside and on an unshaded patio. Almost everything is fried, but that's what fish and chips is about; if you dislike the fat smell, you can take your meal, neatly packed in styrofoam, to eat in Lithia Park. The fish was blah and covered in heavy batter. Prawns and scallops, in the same batter, were slightly tastier. Best were clam strips with a crumb crust. All are served with wedge fries and a choice of coleslaw or pasta salad. The price range is $3.25 for a half order of clam strips to $6.95 for a full combination plate. Chicken strips, salads and beverages are also available.

## ICE CREAM

*Cafe Vanille Ice Cream Parlor*                           *482-9764*
*40 North Main St.*

Good ice cream in cones and a full menu of soda fountain specialties are offered here, plus hamburgers, sandwiches, and espresso coffees. There is seating inside, off the Orchard Valley Mall, or at sidewalk tables in good weather.

*Dairy Queen*
*Siskiyou Boulevard*

Under construction in late 1987, between The Bushes and the Hillside Inn, this is the first franchise so close to the center of town; there's no telling before it opens what will be served besides soft ice cream.

*Gerry's Homemade Ice Cream*                              *482-4591*
*57 North Main St.*

Fine, flavorful ice cream, in cones or dishes, with a distinctive texture much like crank freezers produce and quite different from commercial ice cream. Open in the summer; in winter this space becomes the Pinnacle Orchards Christmas Store.

*Honey Treat Yogurt*                                      *482-9602*
*45 North Main St., on the plaza*

Frozen Yogurt with a peculiar, waxy texture plus Dreyer's ice cream; a short menu of lunches is also available.

*Rich Maid*                                                     *482-2426*
*1630 Siskiyou Blvd. at Walker*

This is much more of a restaurant than you would guess from outside. In addition to the drive-thru window there is a pleasant seating area inside, and the menu offers a variety of burgers, sandwiches, baked potatoes and Mexican items as well as shakes and sundaes. The spiral cut french fries are amusing and the burgers edible if unexciting, but the ice cream is what's special here. They've been making their own, in many flavors, since 1953, and it's delicious.

*Rosie's Sweet Shoppe*                                          *488-0179*
*303 East Main St.*

Rosie's offers the classic soda fountain menu of ice cream specialties and sandwiches. There are lots of sandwich options and combinations available and the results are quite tasty. Hot dogs, bagels and Mexican things are available too. Their own ice cream is outstanding and they also sell candy. Rosie's is a popular after theatre stop.

*Royal Yogurt Shoppe*                                          *482-9271*
*1634 Ashland St., in the Ashland Center*

Unusually good frozen yogurt with many toppings including fresh fruit is the specialty at this shopping center restaurant. The seating area is clean and bright and they offer soup and sandwiches too. If you happen to be near here when you get hungry, you can have a tasty lunch or snack.

Ice Cream Summary: Ashland in summer makes anything frozen taste welcome, but some of the ice cream made here is exceptional by any standard. Rosie's and Rich Maid are both delicious; Gerry's and Cafe Vanille are very good; If you prefer frozen yogurt, Royal Yogurt is good, too. Ice Cream prices are very reasonable; 65 cents for a single cone is typical.

## Miscellaneous Snacks

*Beanery Coffeehouse*
*1602 Ashland St., Highway 66*

A college student hangout serving espresso coffees and desserts.

*Cindy's Espresso*
*199 East Main St.*

Four tables in the crafts gallery serving espresso coffee and snacks.

*Cuppa Joe*
*60 East Main Street*

A coffee and tea store serving espresso and Italian sodas.

*The Juice Bar*
*On the plaza, at the entrance to Rare Earth*

A portable stand dispensing refreshing fruit juices and lemonade.

*Mana From Heaven Bakery*
*358 East Main St.*

Truly heavenly baked goods, from bread to the fanciest pastries, to take out or eat there. They open at 7:30 AM or before and coffee is available to go with the goodies.

*Mr. Popcorn*
*297 East Main Street*

Just popcorn in many improbable flavors; it seems unlikely they can sell enough to survive, so hurry if you like popcorn.

*Mustard's Last Stand*
*On the plaza, in front of Flower Thyme*

Literally, a hole in the wall. If the operator eats too many of his hot dogs he may get stuck.

*Puck's Doughnuts*
*44 C St.*

Lots of different kinds plus drinks to go with them, to eat there or take away. They tend to open and close early; 6 AM to noon is typical.

# *Light Meals*

Listed below are the restaurants that everybody thinks of for breakfast and lunch, but not for dinner, though most of the dinner places in the next two sections also serve lunch, and a few do breakfasts. In fact, many of these coffee shops and delis serve all day, and fortunately for those who are looking for smaller dinners, they often continue to offer eggs and sandwiches and light lunch dishes.

These are the places where nobody minds if you don't want a main course, though they usually have a selection for those who do, and where the cooking is less elaborate than in the traditional dinner restaurants. Most of them serve beer and wine but not hard liquor. Most take credit cards. Ethnic restaurants, Chinese and Mexican in particular, also lend themselves to a la carte dining, but they are listed in a section of their own. For the definition of the price ranges, see page 173.

> *ABC on A Street*             *488-2769*
> *340 A St., #2, iacross from the Grange Co-op.*
> *Breakfast and lunch*
> *Low to moderate prices*

This is the production bakery for the Ashland Bakery Cafe, listed below. Coffee and baked goods, and at lunch time a short list of sandwiches, are available in a bright, blue and white shop decorated with fascinating photographs of the historic district in which it is located.

> *Andre's Restaurant*             *482-5092*
> *1209 Siskiyou, in front of the Valley Entrance Motel*
> *Breakfast, lunch and dinner*
> *Moderate prices*

Big and plastic, but none the less attractive, this coffee shop is very popular for breakfast. In fact, the breakfasts are good but nothing special, and so are the lunch sandwiches. This seems to be the exceptional coffee shop that shines at dinner. Fresh salmon and broccoli crepes were spectacular and they serve prime rib on Friday and Saturday. Portions are moderate and beer and wine are available.

*Ashland Bakery Cafe*          *482-2117*
*38 East Main St., next to the City Hall*
*Breakfast, lunch, Sunday brunch and dinner*
*Prices low to moderate*

Lots of health food and vegetarian dishes, chicken and fish but no meat, and bakery treats of course. Breakfasts are outstanding, but watch out for the heavy whole wheat pastries, the bakery's one failing. Dinner entrees are huge and easily shared, especially if you want to try a dessert. This is a local hangout; you're likely to spot last night's actors at brunch.

*Bee Gee's*          *488-1604*
*1823 Siskiyou Blvd., at the Cedarwood Motel*
*Breakfast, lunch and dinner*
*Low prices*

Bee Gee's is a popular Medford chain of family restaurants. They have opened in the space that was formerly occupied by the Cookhouse, which closed. The menu includes the standard, with omelets and breakfast scombinations, burgers and sandwiches for lunch and inexpensive dinners. The service is friendly but the food is disappointing.

*The Breadboard*          *488-0295*
*744 North Main St.*
*Breakfast (opening at 7 AM) and lunch*
*Low to moderate prices.*

Fabulous breakfasts. The humongous cinnamon rolls now served all over Ashland may have started here. Fresh fruit here is really fresh, often local. Home fries are crisp round slices of fresh potato. This place used to share the building with a wood stove company; the stoves are now relegated to an ad on the back of the menu. The sandwiches and home baked pie for lunch are good too, if not as spectacular as the breakfasts. They also have soup, salads and a daily hot dish.

*Brothers' Restaurant and Delicatessen*     *482-9671*
*95 North Main St., just north of the plaza*

*Breakfast (from 7 AM), Lunch and Dinner (closing at 8 PM)*
*Prices generally moderate, low for dinners*

This is Ashland's version of a New York deli, but it's a long way from here to Seventh Avenue. For breakfast there are eggs and bacon and huevos rancheros along with lox and eggs and potato pancakes. Besides deli meat sandwiches they do coffee shop standards and hamburgers for lunch, and their dinner entrees are equally diverse. Everything on the menu is available all day and can be packed in special boxes to take away.

*The Copper Skillet*         482-2684
*2270 Ashland St., almost to the freeway interchange*
*Breakfast (from 6 AM, 7 AM on Sundays), lunch and dinner*
*Moderate prices, low for dinners*

Breakfast is served all day and is clearly the thing to have. Omelets in amazing variety are the specialty; they're huge but good. There is a little salad bar with about twenty five crocks with all the standard things, the hamburgers are delicious, and the pies home made. Dinner entrees here are not so reliable.

*The Eatery*         482-8555
*58 East Main St., with an entrance from the Festival courtyard, too*
*Breakfast, lunch and dinner*
*Low to moderate prices*

The perfectly decent food here is handicapped by a relentlessly cute menu. Every dish has a theatrical name and the jokes aren't very funny. Hamlet's Honor — chicken breast — was nicely flavored with thyme and lemon and the accompaniments were pleasant enough, too. The decor is a bit fussy, with too many plants and patterns, and the service can be slow when they're crowded, but the location is unbeatable.

*Greenleaf Grocery and Delicatessen*         482-2808
*49 North Main, opposite the plaza*
*Currently open 9 AM to 9 PM*
*Low to moderate prices*

Don't be put off by the line; it moves fast and when you reach the front you'll have your meal, on a tray to carry out to their two level deck overlooking the creek, or skillfully packed to go. There are also a few booths inside. You can choose a sandwich off the menu boards and it will be made as you progress toward the cash register. Delicious hot dishes (some vegetarian), salads, and desserts, are displayed for your selection, and drinks are in refrigerated cases. A number of local products are featured here, including Pyramid juices and truffles made by the Reinhardts of Cowslip's Belle. This place is a real winner.

> *Hall of Fame Restaurant*                              *488-0111*
> *2510 Hwy. 66, next to the Flagship Quality Inn*
> *Open 24 hours every day*
> *Low prices*

Basic freeway coffee shop with acceptable food; at 4 AM it's this or groceries from Safeway if you don't feel like driving out of town. If you don't mind a few miles on I-5, The Pear Tree is substantially nicer *(sww page 209)*.

> *Main Street Deli*                              *482-4350*
> *272 East Main St.*
> *Low to moderate prices*

This is a cheerful sandwich shop decorated with stenciled folk patterns and run by very pleasant people. If you happen to be in the area at lunch time, you can get a quick and acceptable lunch here.

> *Munchies*                              *488-2967*
> *59 North Main, downstairs from Gerry's Ice Cream*
> *Breakfast, lunch and early dinners*
> *Moderate prices, low for dinners*

Munchies is located in a basement; given the inherently unappealing location, they have made it quite attractive. There is a bakery where the pies are deeper, the rolls larger than anywhere else, and a restaurant with giant portions too. Breakfast is served all day, and there are burgers and sandwiches. Highly individual versions of Mexican dishes are the specialty and they're tasty if not authentic.

> *Oak Tree Restaurant and Lounge*                              *488-1434*
> *2365 Highway 66, at the I-5 interchange*
> *Open 6 AM to midnight, every day*
> *Prices low to moderate*

Another freeway coffee shop, but with good cinnamon rolls and croissants for breakfast and a windowless bar with sports on the TV.

*The Safeway (grocery store) Deli*          482-5315
*585 Siskiyou Blvd.*
*Low prices*

Safeway has a big deli department with people available to make sandwiches to order. There is a salad bar and a pot of hot soup. With what you can find in the produce department and the bakery, and maybe some wine, you can put together quite a picnic here. The store is open 24 hours every day, but the deli won't have everything out in the middle of the night.

*The Sandwich Shack*          482-5767
*On Siskiyou at the corner of Avery, near SOSC*
*Open 10 AM to 6 PM, 4 PM on Saturdays, closed Sundays*
Low to moderate prices

You design your own sandwich here, choosing up to three items from a list of meats and cheeses plus the kind of roll and sauce you want and they make it, with lettuce, tomato and onion, too. There's a limited menu of salads and garnishes and cold drinks, including beer and wine, to complete your lunch. All the food is packed to go, but there are tables if you want to eat it there. The Shack is aimed at the college students, but it's sometimes convenient for visitors to be able to get a picnic lunch without fighting the crowds downtown. These sandwiches are a bargain; they make them in three sizes, from $2.25 to $4.50, but the small one is a hearty lunch, and a side of soup or salad adds only fifty cents to the bill.

*Stagedoor Sidewalk Cafe*          488-2779
*120 East Main*
*Lunch and dinner*
*Low to moderate prices*

This is an attractive little place next door to the Black Swan Theatre, with a few tables inside and a few more on a terrace. They offer omelets, burgers, and a few inexpensive entrees and specialize in sandwiches topped with melted cheese. Unfortunately they don't know how to cook them; I was served wet tuna salad on a soggy muffin with cold, stiff cheese, which I simply couldn't eat.

*Toonerville Deli Depot*          482-1233
*In the Orchard Lane Mall, on North Main St.*

This is a basic sandwich place. I watched the man behind the counter spread the tuna on my sandwich with his finger. That is sufficiently beyond the normal amount of handling of the ingredients of a sandwich that I am unable to tell you how it tasted.

*Underground Deli*                                  *488-2595*
*125 East Main, below Paddington Station, or off the alley*
*Breakfast, Lunch and Dinner (till 8 PM, 4 PM Sunday and Monday)*
*Low to moderate prices*

The London underground is the theme here, though the sign painter who did up the walk in refrigerator door as the back of a departing train made it look more like a San Francisco cable car. Inventive omelets, waffles, sandwiches and salads are served all day and packed to go. Half sandwiches and small side orders make creating little meals easy here, and the desserts are great.

# Ethnic Food

When you need a change there are a few treasures here, and some good sources of light meals as well. The price ranges are explained on page 173.

## CHINESE

*China Station*                    488-0101
*2425 Siskiyou, almost at the southern edge of town*
*Lunch and dinner at moderate prices*

Don't mind the tiny shack; it's bigger and nicer inside than you'd guess. A serious young man is the host here; his wife, who is from China, and another chef do the cooking. They are proud of the authentic ingredients they use and the unusual Szechuan and Hunan dishes they offer along with more usual Cantonese ones. They will leave out the MSG if you ask, but can't guarantee that some of the imported sauces they use don't contain it. The food here is well worth the trek out Siskiyou Blvd.; the homemade barbecued pork is particularly good.

*Dahlia Restaurant*                    482-5059
*29 North Main St., on the plaza*
*Lunch, except Monday, and Dinner*
*Moderate prices*

The Dahlia has been here since 1966. The location is great, the decor is traditional restaurant-Chinese, they don't use MSG, but the cooking is tired. They offer a lot of fried things, especially on the combination plates, and also make American dishes.

*Golden Dynasty*                                    *488-0077*
*1415 Siskiyou, just past the Highway 66 turnoff, near SOSC*
*Lunch and dinner, seven days a week*
*Moderate prices*

Again, combination plates of fried food and an American menu. The Golden Dynasty is bright and new, and has pleasant-enough dishes with fresh vegetables if you can avoid the deep fried things. However, it isn't distinguished cooking.

## ITALIAN

*Gepetto's*                                         *482-1138*
*345 East Main St.*
*Breakfast (from 8 AM) lunch and dinner (to midnight)*
*Low to moderate prices*

Gepetto's is a friendly local hangout with an Italian accent. It isn't quiet or elegant, and the cooking isn't fancy, but a wide variety of tasty dishes is available, from burgers and stuffed baked potatoes to pasta, steak and fish dinners. There are vegetarian options on the menu — in fact, they grow their own organic produce.

*Little Caesar's*                                   *482-4561*
*1253 Siskiyou, near the college*
*Breakfast, lunch and dinner (no dinners on Sunday)*
*Low prices*

The breakfast and lunch menus are standard American coffee shop, well-enough cooked and pleasant tasting, but unremarkable. At night Little Caesar's turns Italian with considerable flair, especially given the prices. Pasta, chicken and fish dishes are served in reasonably sized portions along with salad and vegetables. Wine and beer are available and the food is really quite nice.

## MEXICAN

*Cesar's*                                           *482-1107*
*76 North Pioneer, just below Main St.*
*Lunch (in summer only) and dinner*
*Very low prices*

This is a pretty upstairs room with arched booths and colorful flowers

Festival dancers gather around the Elizabethan Theatre sign during 40th anniversary celebrations. *Oregon Shakespearean Festival, photo by Hank Kranzler.*

painted on the walls. The most expensive dinner is under $5, they give special discounts to seniors, and they have a folk singer entertaining during dinner. There is the full range of Mexican dishes, with nothing fried, they assure you, and beer or wine. The food isn't spicy at all, nor is it authentically Mexican, or Tex-Mex for that matter, but it is quite good and certainly cheap.

> *La Burrita*                          *482-0813, 488-2233*
> *397 East Main St.*
> *Low prices*

Here you order your food and pay at the counter, and then help yourself to chips and salsa and sit in a huge roomful of tables with pinatas and blankets hanging everywhere. The space is very jolly so it's a pity the food is so totally without flavor, never mind spice. I know everything Mexican isn't hot, but this is ridiculous.

> *Taco Bell*                          *488-2604*
> *2290 Ashland St, near the I-5 interchange*
> The fast food version.

189

## EXOTIC

*Immigrant Restaurant*          482-2547
*19 First St., just below Main St.*
*Dinner, from 5 PM to 8 PM*
*Low to very moderate prices*

The lunch counter and small dining room here are entertainingly decorated with artifacts from Afghanistan — clothing, jewelry, post cards, maps and posters. The dinners aren't likely to become your daily fare, but they make an interesting change of pace. Braised meats, rice, spinach and yogurt are major ingredients, and the flat, chewy bread is not to be missed.

*Thai Pepper — Some Like It Hot*          482-8058
*84 North Main St.*

The Beasy's/Back Porch/Change of Heart Empire has announced their next venture which will be located in the same block as the Back Porch BBQ, downstairs from the Hanson Howard Gallery. If you look over the railing you can see an attractive deck built out over the creek. It should be open by the time you read this, if you like incendiary Asian food.

# Dinners

These are the places that (with a few exceptions) take reservations and accept credit cards and expect you to eat a meal at dinner-time, not a snack. That doesn't mean that all of them are formal or fancy, though all of them do have some indefinable quality that makes them restaurants, not coffee shops. Most of these places are also open for lunch, and about a third serve breakfast, too.

At dinner, the price of the entree typically includes your choice of soup or salad, occasionally both. Wine and beer, and usually cocktails, are available. For details on the price ranges, see page 173.

> *Alex's Plaza Restaurant and Bar*                          *482-8818*
> *35 N. Main, on the plaza*
> *Lunch, brunch on Sunday, dinner, and after theatre snacks.*
> *Prices are moderate to expensive.*

Alex's opened this year in a light and spacious loft above a group of stores on the plaza, across from the fountain. A flight of stairs enclosed in leafy ironwork takes you to one of the handsomest restaurant spaces in town, all pink brick and dark green wallpaper. In front, there is a long, traditional bar, tables overlooking the plaza and soft chairs around a fireplace for cocktails. The dining area, in the rear, is bright and airy, with comfortable banquettes and well separated tables, and there is additional seating on a deck overlooking the creek.

Alex deserves great praise for accurately restoring a boringly modernized building to its whimsical, 1905 glory. The picture on page 6 shows a before picture of flat redwood siding and small windows that contributed nothing to the Plaza like the charm of the new balcony and columns and cool green paint. The only thing lacking now is food as good as the architecture.

The menus are brief and full of fashionably complex and spicy dishes but the results are disappointing. At the height of the summer growing season a six dollar fruit salad ought to include more than melon, pineapple and grapes. Home fried potatoes and cut fruit garnishes ought to be fresh and crisp no matter what time you come for brunch. At a

The building that now houses Alex's resturant as it looked circa 1909. *Ashland Public Library, print by Terry Skib*

restaurant of this quality all the food ought to be freshly prepared, not reheated. Alex's is such an attractive place, and the staff is so pleasant and helpful, that I hope the problems in the kitchen prove to be short-lived.

*The Back Porch BBQ*                                          *482-4131*
*92 1/2 North Main St., just north of the plaza*
*Lunch and dinner, closed in winter*
*Very moderate prices*

The designer of this restaurant should win an award for creativity, for making an amusing place out of nothing but a basement and the vacant lot next door. You come down a covered staircase from the street and sit at tables scattered over decks and level spaces on the sloped lot. When the BBQ first opened you stood in line and filed through the basement kitchen to collect your food; perhaps that was too authentic, as it's been changed to waitress service.

The menu is basically barbecued meats, chicken and shrimp, which can be ordered singly or in combinations, and in regular or large portions. Two side dishes are included, your choice of salads, beans, or potato chips. The whole meal comes in a compartmented picnic plate, topped with a slab of really home-made tasting bread. Cold drinks of all sorts, including alcoholic, are available, as are special salads for those who don't want barbecue.

The style is supposed to be Texan, and it certainly is back yard informal, complete with some flies and yellow jackets for company. The barbecue, particularly the shrimp and chicken, is very tasty, and the sauce is not terribly hot. This is an easy place to take children.

*Beasy's Back Room*                                         *482-2141*
*139 East Main St., upstairs, in back of Change of Heart*
*Dinner, 5 PM to 10 PM*
*Low to moderate prices*

Another informal, western style restaurant by the owners of the Back Porch BBQ, this one specializes in grilled meats, sausages, chicken, shrimp and fish. Meals include an unusual green salad, with chopped tomatos and green olives, and fried wedges of potato. The food is usually very good, and there is a full bar in addition to wine and beer.

The room is the leftover space behind Change of Heart, a high, brick walled loft that is furnished with simple wooden chairs and tables. There are furry potted cacti, neon beer signs and a few old west artifacts for decor; my favorite is a collection of all the forms barbed wire came in.

There are a couple of special deals available here, but you have to ask for them. Between five and six, early birds can have the small sirloin steak dinner, regularly $7.65, with grilled onions and your choice of drinks from the bar, for $6. After the play starts, at either eight or eight-thirty, the same thing is available except that the drink is limited to beer or wine.

*Cascade Dining Room* 482-8310
*Ashland Hills Inn*
*2525 Ashland St.(Hwy. 66), at the I-5 interchange*
*Full range of prices, low to expensive*

The Ashland Hills Inn advertises that their dining room is a bit better than the average motel coffee shop, and I'd have to agree. For one thing, the tiered space overlooking the tennis area and garden is unusually handsome. Also, they put a lot of effort into service and presentation, and the food is pretty good, too.

The breakfast menu features all the usual things, but the fresh fruit I ordered came as a layered compote of berries and banana in red white and blue. For lunch there are sandwiches and salads, of course, and pleasant tables on the deck at which to eat them. At dinner time there are a variety of small-meal options available, and there is pleasant live music.

The Sunday brunch is one of those giant buffets where you are tempted to eat too much, with seating in an interior room that is not so pleasant. There also seems to be a shortage of non smoking tables. Aside from these minor points, the Cascade Room seems to live up to its billing.

*Change of Heart* 488-0235
*139 East Main St., upstairs*
*Dinner, reservations essential in summer,*
*Expensive*

This is the third of the Beasy/Back Porch group of restaurants, but it is as sleek and formal as they are casual. The brick loft space it shares with Beasy's looks entirely different with table cloths and potted plants and coppery blinds covering the tall windows. The view from those windows, of the houses and festival buildings on the hillside in the late afternoon sunshine, is a memorable one.

Unfortunately, there are several tables in the front hall that share none of this elegant ambiance and have uncomfortably high, wooden seats.

You should ask where your table will be and refuse to sit in the hall unless you are immune to feeling like the unwanted stepchild.

The menu here is entirely a la carte, with a selection of starters, entrees and desserts that is changed weekly. The dishes are imaginative and more nearly nouvelle or California in style than classic French. Though not every preparation is equally successful, the level of both cooking and presentation is generally high. I have had wonderful food here, particularly soups and salads, and disasters, most recently an overage, overcooked duck.

I can understand an occasional poor dish; every restaurant goofs sometime, especially if the menu is inventive. What I can't forgive is the increasing air of hauteur, as if they were doing you some great favor letting you eat there. My impression is that the number of less than perfect dishes is increasing and that the service is getting slower and less careful. Don't put up with it for a moment — I should have sent my duck back, so they'd know I wasn't fooled — they can do better here.

They have a good selection of wines, by the glass as well as in bottles. As at Beasy's, you have to ask for the special deal, which is two dinners for the price of one for late diners.

*Chateaulin Restaurant and Cafe*         *482-2264*
*50 East Main St., next to the ramp from the festival*
*Dinner and after theatre snacks until the bar closes*
*Reservations essential*
*Prices moderate (cafe menu) to expensive*

Chateaulin has been going now for about fifteen years in this same little space. It's intimate and charming, with dark wood and a brick wall with some of the ivy coming through on the inside, and dark blue cushions. Recently a second dining room has been opened in a windowless space behind the shop next door. It is less crowded but somewhat bare by contrast. A hot and busy night can be a little overpowering here as the air conditioning can't quite keep up with the heat and cigarette smoke, and the noise level can get high.

The food is French, well cooked and deftly served. On Mondays, and other days after eight, an a la carte cafe menu of smaller dishes is available, and some of the first courses and desserts continue to be available after ten. The wine list is extensive, with about a dozen varieties available by the glass and a selection of endangered vintages offered with no price

195

specified. (I suspect drinking the last of something is expensive.) The dessert menu includes a long and inventive list of drinks combining espresso coffee or steamed milk and liqueurs.

Chateaulin is about as fancy as dining in Ashland gets, and the food really is worth getting out of your jeans for.

> *Gamekeeper's Inn*                                        482-2293
> *568 East Main St., borderline for walking, down a few stairs*
> *Breakfast, lunch and dinner*
> *Moderate prices*

The craftsman bungalow that used to be the Clark Cottage Restaurant has taken on a new identity. This isn't where you got the moose steaks; the game here is Monopoly or Chess or Trivial Pursuit, used as decoration and also available for customers to play. Except for the new theme, the dining room looks much as it did before, and there are still umbrella tables in the garden, though I'm told a new look is planned.

At least one dish on the menu is a holdover from the Clark Cottage, too. Hopplepopple, an unusual meat and potato scramble, was a breakfast specialty then and is still available. Lunches feature grilled sandwiches now, with soups and salads. The entrees available at dinner include steak, chicken teriyaki, grilled halibut, spaghetti, mixed vegetable sautes and spanakopita, the spinach-and-cheese-filled Greek pastries. The entrees come with delicious salad, and the desserts are homemade and very good.

Both the design of some of the dishes served here and the execution reveal new-restaurant problems, but they are already making changes. For example, the substantial lunch sandwiches were originally garnished with fried potatoes or pasta salad and now a lighter choice, tossed greens, is available too. Most of the food is good and the staff is eager to please; when they've had time to get things running smoothly, this ought to be a very interesting place.

> *Jazmin's*                                        488-0883
> *180 C St., a block below East Main*
> *Dinner and late snacks (to 2:30 PM some evenings)*
> *Low to moderate prices*

Jazmin's is mostly known as a night club these days, though it was once a popular Middle Eastern restaurant. It's a big, multi-level place, paneled

196

in wood and feeling rather dark if it's still sunny outside as there are no windows. There's a bar and a dance floor near the stage, and several areas with tables.

The menu contains mostly contemporary American standards now — broiled fish and chicken and steak — but a couple of exotic specialties are still offered. I had read reports that the food was no longer good, but the Bastachi, filo packages of chicken and mushrooms with Armenian seasoning, were as tasty as ever.

They serve drinks and wine and exotic coffees with liqueurs, and several of their dishes, including the Bastachi, are available in appetizer portions for eating during the shows. The service was friendly, but very slow; I got the impression they didn't expect early diners, though the food was certainly worth coming for, with or without a show to see.

*Jonathan's*                                           482-0049
*182 North Main St., at the Bard's Inn*
*Breakfast, lunch and dinner, reserve for dinner*
*Moderate to expensive*

Jonathan's is another new restaurant, but it shows no sign of hesitant first steps. The dinner menu here is focused on seafood prepared in various contemporary ways. A choice of unusual soups or a green salad, with which several different vinaigrette dressings are offered, is included in the price of the entree. The dramatic presentation of the deserts, with multiple sauces in patterns on the plate, ends the meal in high style.

The bar at Jonathan's serves only wine, but nearly everything on the wine list is available by the glass. A single glass is often all you want before going to a play, and it's fun to have so many different wines to choose from.

Bard's Inn was recently purchased by chef Jonathan Warren and is undergoing a renovation of which the new restaurant is part. The triangular space has been decorated in subtle desert colors, with the wine bar in the point. With its bands of windows overlooking the town, it is a handsome room in which to dine.

Jonathan's is also the motel coffee shop for breakfast and lunch, a role in which it performs with far less competence. Though the room is, if anything, lovelier in the morning sunshine, breakfast there was disappointing: a small selection of dishes, competently cooked but hardly inspired. The service was slow and amateurish, but both that and the dull food may well improve with time.

> *North Light*                                            *482-9463*
> *36 South Second St.*
> *Breakfast, lunch and dinner*
> *Low prices*

North Light is across the street from and a wonderful contrast to the Winchester Inn. The front rooms of an old house have been simply remodeled into a light, square space that is furnished with modern oak tables and chairs. The windows are draped with multicolored layers of dyed cheesecloth and there are misty, rainbow colored pictures on the walls.

This is a strictly vegetarian restaurant; no eggs or dairy products are used, though you can ask for cheese. Breakfast dishes include cereals and tofu scrambles, and there are soups, sandwiches, salads and homemade muffins. Dinners with various entrees, many of them Mexican in inspiration, include soup and salad; you can have beer or wine if you wish. I didn't like all the food here equally, but it has lots of flavor and it's definitely different.

"Someday," the waitress said to me, "People are going to say that the Winchester Inn is across from North Light."

> *The Oak Knoll Restaurant*                               *482-4312*
> *3070 Highway 66, at the golf course, just beyond the freeway*
> *Lunch and dinner*
> *Moderate to expensive prices*

Lunches here are standard salads and sandwiches, very nicely made but nothing out of the ordinary. The great thing is the setting with its lawns and oak trees. Eating out on the deck is so serene, such a tranquil change from downtown Ashland and the Festival, that a good meal is almost just a nice bonus. The deck overlooks a green where golfers practice putting, and it's entertaining to watch them struggle.

At night, the menu is steak and roast beef and seafood, served in a variety of surf and turf combinations as well as separately. The dining room looks type-cast for a golf club and there is also a small but attractive bar.

*Omar's*          *482-1281*
*1380 Siskiyou Blvd., near where highway 66 turns off*
*Lunch (weekdays only) and dinner*
*All price ranges, but mostly moderate*
*No reservations, and the line forms early*

Omar's is named after the original chef-owner who started a roadside steak house here in 1946. The booths in the non-smoking area still have those Seeburg record selectors, for operating the jukebox from your table, though they don't work anymore. The main dining room is an addition in an entirely different style, all dim lights and red leatherette.

Steaks and seafood are the specialties at Omar's. Dinners include a salad you serve yourself from a sort of portable salad bar, a bowl of greens with compartments for garnishes around the base. A choice of interesting salad dressings and a basket of hot wheat bread come with the salad. The spectacularly light fried zucchini fingers and onion rings are wonderful with it too, though there are more conventional appetizers on the menu. The size of the dinners makes it hard to think about dessert here, but they're also fine.

It's easy to forget how good simple food can be. Omar's is a personal favorite. The people are nice and the service competent even when it's crowded, and there are plenty of things on the menu that aren't fancified. It's still a first class roadside steak house, complete with bar.

*Tommy's*          *482-3556*
*47 North Main St., on the plaza*
*Breakfast (from 8 AM), lunch, Sunday brunch and dinner*
*Low to moderate prices*

If you're returning to Ashland after a few years away and looking for the Lithia Grocery, this is where it was, but all that's left are the funny slat benches that slide you forward, just like the ones on the old San Francisco ferries. Otherwise, no trace of laid back hippie atmosphere remains in this crisply contemporary restaurant and bar.

The menus include an eclectic mixture of dishes, all done with considerable style. Lennie's Special, poached eggs and jack cheese on English muffins, is a good alternative to the usual breakfast plates, and several kinds of French toast are also offered. There are more brunch choices here than at Alex's down the block, and lower prices. Dinner options range from steak and fish to Lasagna, Mexican dishes and sandwiches.

This is a good place to bring children. The booths are big, there is lots to choose from on the menu and the atmosphere is pleasantly relaxed; nobody's going to be too bothered by a little noise or spilled milk here.

*The Winchester Inn*                                                   *488-1115*
*35 South Second, at Hargadine*
*Sunday brunch and dinner (closed Monday)*
*Reservatios recommended for both*
*Expensive*

The Winchester Inn occupies a large Victorian house that is on the National Register of Historic Places. Several main floor rooms overlooking the terraced hillside garden are used for dining, along with tables on the patio. The decor is all pale gray with lace curtains and wine colored carpet, a very sleek, updated version of Victorian. There is a Siberia here, too, across the hall, where an occasional party dines in lonely splendor; unless your group is large enough to generate it's own cheer, you should decline a table there.

The Sunday brunch menu offers standard dishes with individual touches: apple pancakes made with whole wheat flour, a creamed seafood dish that includes smoked oysters, french toast coated with almonds. They do breakfasts well and the room is exceptionally pretty in the morning light.

Dinners are quite elaborate. A choice of Cultivator's Soup, a clear tomato vegetable with parmesan that is a specialty here, or the soup du jour, is followed by a green salad, both included with the entree. There is a list of tempting first courses too; it's unfortunate the menu is not set up for ordering a la carte as interesting light meals could be made by combining an appetizer with soup or salad and a dessert. The entrees are all sauced and served with vegetables and garnishes.

Like Change of Heart, the Winchester Inn has a record of mixed success and failure and a tendency to pretentious service. If I have a general complaint about the food it is that nothing is plain, but this is a very festive restaurant, and the complexity of the dishes certainly contributes to the sense of occasion.

# Out of Town

I doubt any place in rural America could win even one star from the Guide Michelin's inspectors, but on the roads around Ashland you can find restaurants that are, in Michelin's words, worth a detour, at least by American standards. Some that I've listed below are close enough for dinner before a play; others are farther and better suited to being part of a day's exploration away from Ashland. All offer both good meals and a change of scene.

This is a list of some old family favorites, and some new discoveries. Outside of Ashland I couldn't try every single restaurant, and in this list I've also omitted the places I tried and didn't like.

> *Applegate River House*           *846-6810*
> *15100 Hwy 238, Applegate*
> *Dinner, and Sunday brunch*
> *Moderate prices*

Sitting on the deck of this modern, rustic restaurant, you're close enough to see the big fish swimming up the Applegate River. There are three long, family-style tables out on the deck and more smaller ones inside, several with a nice view of the river, too. Brunch outside, on a sunny Sunday, is well worth taking the pretty drive through Jacksonville and Ruch; it's about twenty five miles from Ashland.

There are unusual choices on the brunch menu, Spanakopita and a ground beef and spinach scramble as well as Eggs Benedict and French Toast, and they'll serve the child's portion to anyone with a small appetite. Dinner choices include various pastas, fish such as fresh salmon, chicken and steak. Wine and beer are served and desserts are a specialty.

The location is idyllic, the service is both friendly and competent, and the food is excellent. You could combine a meal here with a visit to Jacksonville, or stop at Valley View Vineyards, or continue on Hwy. 238 to Grants Pass.

*Arbor House*                                                    *535-6817*
*105 West Wagner, Talent*
*Dinner, Wednesday (Thursday in winter) through Sunday*
*Moderate prices, especially for this food*

Talent is a town of no visible planning or control, seemingly as loose as Ashland, its neighbor to the south, is tightly regulated. To get to Arbor House from Ashland you go north on Highway 99. When you get to Talent, take a left at the lights and go a block or so to the end of the street, where you'll see Jittery-Joe's-Buy-Sell-Trade, and go left again. Then make a quick right at the bar and pool hall and go a couple of blocks till you cross the railroad tracks. On your left you'll see a handsome wooden sign in front of a blue mobile home with a vine and lattice front porch. Park in the weedy dirt yard and ignore everything outside the arbor; inside is the very special world of Patrick and Kitty.

Arbor House has been here by the tracks for eight years and I regret deeply not knowing about it for the first seven. The food is quite wonderful and the chef-owners will give you samples if you're dubious about choosing a dish or concerned that a curry may be too spicy. Curries are a specialty, but so are sauerbraten served with all the German trimmings, and any number of other international dishes. Each will be lovingly explained by either Patrick or Kitty and cooked and ceremoniously served by them, too. It's a process that takes time and is worth it. They love food and wine and it's a pleasure to eat with them.

*Bel Di's on the Rogue*                                          *878-2010*
*Highway 62, Shady Cove*
*Dinner*
*Moderate prices*

Shady Cove is about twenty miles north of Medford, or about thirty five from Ashland. Bel Di's is on your right, going north, a bit beyond what seems to be the main intersection; this is a town without a center. There is a large landscaped parking lot, and behind it in the trees, a complex of low, brown buildings. Inside you will find a full bar, and past that, a long dining room that overlooks the river.

The food here is only slightly Italian in style. Dinners include both soup and salad, and both were above average. There are various seafood entrees as well as veal dishes, chicken and steak — nothing too unusual, but nicely cooked and presented. The dessert selection was limited, mostly ice cream.

I ended up here after a day at the lakes east of Ashland and a visit to the old mill at Eagle Point. It might also make a good stop on the road back from a day at Crater Lake. The dining room is handsome, elegant without being stuffy, a nice restful finish to an active day out-of-doors.

> *Callahan's Siskiyou Lodge*                          *482-1299*
> *at the Mt. Ashland exit from I-5*
> *Dinner*
> *Low to moderate prices*

Callahan's, in spite of the name, is an Italian restaurant. It's a huge, rustic, ski lodge sort of place below the freeway; if you're coming from Ashland you have to turn back under the freeway to find it.

The dinners here are immense and follow the traditional pattern of family-style Italian meals. The antipasto of marinated beans, olives, peppers. carrot and celery sticks and salami is routine, but the whipped cheese-butter and sesame bread sticks it comes with are not. That cheese spread is the least resistible thing since salted peanuts. The soup is a good home style minestrone, full of beans and vegetables. The salad is crisp and light and is served with warm bread that brings out the garlic in the cheese spread. Then there is spaghetti, of course, and the entree you've chosen, and last, spumoni or ice cream with creme de menthe sauce, and coffee.

Entrees include big steaks, fried chicken, veal, prawns and pasta dishes. If all this seems vastly more food than you want to face there are ways to reduce it. For one thing, ordering pasta effectively skips the entree and the spaghetti, too. And there is also that most ambiguous of menu entries, "a la carte service charge $5," which turns out to be the charge for sharing an entree. You can eat all you want of the first courses and have dessert and coffee, a pretty good deal.

Callahan's is a cheerful, friendly place with a bar and a big deck to wait on with your drink if the dining room is crowded. The view of endless trees and mountains is very pleasant and the food is just the sort to please most children.

Chata                                                          535-2575
1212 Highway 99, Talent
Dinner
Moderate prices

Chata, which is pronounced "hotta," is a Polish restaurant that also serves two other, weirdly disparate, cuisines: Chicago style deep dish pizza and Cajun specialties like blackened fish. The Polish dishes are unusual and delicious, but I've never tried the pizza (it may make it possible to bring unadventurous children here) and I dislike Cajun spices too much to judge any Cajun dish fairly. But if you want a quick trip to central Europe before a play, this is a great place.

The dining rooms are in an old house (the name means cottage) and the decorations are Polish weavings, some of which are for sale in the entryway. The ambience is warm and the service very good — they will get you out in time for your play if you warn them when you come. Liquor is available as well as wine and beer and they serve half portions of some of the entrees, and wonderful desserts.

Greensprings Inn                                              482-0614
11470 Hwy 66, Ashland
Breakfast, lunch and dinner
Low to moderate prices

It's about twenty miles along the road to Klamath Falls to get to the Greensprings Inn, a log building by the side of the road with an incongruous lighted display case full of desserts set into the front wall. The drive through the forest is peaceful and the views back into the valley are splendid, especially at sunset.

Breakfast here is a bargain, with a wide range of dishes available from egg and meat standards to shrimp omelets. The lunch menu includes burgers, sandwiches and Mexican things, with some vegetarian options. Dinner is Italian, though the soup was a most unusual Mexican Potato the night I dined there. Soup and a huge salad garnished with marinated vegetables are included in the dinners. Entrees are mostly pastas, with a wide variety of sauces, which can also be ordered a la carte, and there are bigger versions of the salad, too. Desserts turn out to be worth showcasing, but you may have trouble if you've eaten everything that comes before.

Greensprings is tied with Arbor House as my favorite discovery.

Very early bus service as shown on a postcard. *Southern Oregon Historical Society.*

*Harry and David's Original Country Store*      *776-2277*
*2836 Highway 99, Medford*
*Breakfast and Lunch, 6 AM to 6 PM*
*Prices low to moderate*

This is an attractive complex of shops. You can buy produce, including those famous pears when they're in season, and local people say the prices are reasonable. They also sell specialty foods and wine, including Harry and David products, delicatessen sandwiches, gifts and Jackson Perkins roses. The packing plant tours (they ship fruit all over) start here, too, so it's good for more than just a meal.

Breakfast, served until 11 AM, includes several $1.99 specials and waffles with fresh fruit as well as the traditional egg and meat combinations, omelets and pancakes . The lunch menu contains an interesting selection of salads and sandwiches plus a few hot dishes that would make good early dinners. Nothing too out of the ordinary, but very well done.

During the summer a dinner cabaret was offered here on five weekends for $19.95 for both dinner and the show. The pianist was playing for lunch the day I came, contributing to the pleasant atmosphere.

205

*Jacksonville Inn*           *899-1900*
*175 E. California St., Jacksonville*
Sunday brunch, lunch and dinner
All price ranges, depending when and where you eat

The inn is a Gold Rush era brick building that has been restored. Upstairs are eight bedrooms; on the main floor there is a souvenir shop in addition to a grand, period dining room; and in the basement there is another dining room and also the bar. The food service here is as complex as some of the dishes.

Breakfast is just for the hotel guests, except for Sunday brunch, which features the usual elaborate dishes and is served in the elegant dining room. Lunch is also served there. At dinner time, two menus are available. The Bistro menu, which is served in the pitch dark basement bar, gives you a long list of entrees which come with bread, a salad and vegetables. These dinners are a nice size and a very nice price. The service is a little vague, and you have to eat by touch or bring a flashlight, but the cooking is good.

The dinner menu is much more elaborate, with many courses and high prices. That may be just what you want for a celebratory dinner, but you may not get to eat it in the handsome, main floor room. I admit I'm prejudiced about dark, low basements, but I would be offended to find myself dining at these prices in a brick cellar while a private party enjoyed the glamorous, airy room upstairs. If they served the bistro food in the basement dining room, instead of in the even darker and closer bar, and the pricey dinners upstairs, it would make more sense. So ask before you make your plans.

*Marin's Cafe*           *535-2911*
*109 Talent Highway, 5.5 miles north on Hwy. 99*
*Breakfast (from 6 AM), lunch and dinner (to 7 PM); closed Sunday*
*Low prices*

This is a plain little place on the main street of Talent, a block off the highway. From Ashland, you turn left at the light and left again; Marin's shares a parking lot with Hairy Larry's barber shop (this is free spirited Talent). At lunch, late in the fall, Marin's was full of local people when most places in Ashland were half empty, and the waitresses knew everyone's name. The menu is absolutely standard coffee shop, but both the cooking and the service are outstanding. It's a great spot for an early breakfast and for snacking — the pie is homemade.

*Paradise Ranch Inn*                479-4333
*7000 Monument Dr., Grants Pass*
*Dinner*
*Expensive*

The white board fences surrounding Paradise Ranch suggest a very leisured sort of ranching — you'd be surprised to see a cow scratching against anything so pristine. The Inn is a resort with facilities for golf and tennis and rooms that overlook a pond with swans. Only at dinner is the restaurant open to non-residents, and it retains a certain clubby atmosphere; it's also dressier than most places hereabouts, but it's not at all snooty.

There are two dining rooms, and the non-smokers get the better of them, a glass walled pavilion with views of the sunset over the water and the mountains in the distance. Dinners can be ordered a la carte or with two additional courses, to be chosen from soup, salad or dessert. Entrees are not unusual — seafood, steak, rack of lamb, veal and chicken — but the ingredients are top quality and the cooking expert. The salad was garnished with shrimp and the vegetable was baked fresh acorn squash when I went, and the wedge fries were sprinkled with parmesan cheese, all nice little touches that make a dinner special. Both drinks and wine are available.

Paradise Ranch is between forty-five and fifty miles from Ashland, at the Merlin exit from I-5, which is just north of Grants Pass. The trick to finding it is turning right at the light and driving parallel to the freeway, rather than going on into Merlin. It's a handsome stretch of country along the freeway or the Rogue River Highway, or you could possibly stop here for dinner on the way back from Oregon Caves.

*The Pear Tree*                535-3372
*At I-5 exit #24, between Ashland and Medford*
*Open 24 hours every day*
*Moderate prices*

If you have a kid who's into trucks, you have to come here. It's a superdeluxe truckstop, and the size and variety of the monsters in the parking area is awesome. Truckers are referred to here as "our professional drivers" and all kinds of services are available for them including a part of the dining room that is reserved with "yield" signs.

The food is basic coffee shop, but it's good, and served with some style, and the dining room is very attractive. In addition to the usual egg breakfasts and sandwich lunches and steak dinners, all available around the clock, there is an all-you-can-eat buffet with the makings of deli sandwiches plus soup and a few desserts. At $4.45, including one beverage, this is a great answer for bottomless teenagers.

*Plymale Cottage*                                                               *899-8807*
*180 N.Oregon, Jacksonville*
*Lunch*
*Moderate prices*

Light lunches are served in several rooms and on the front porch of this 1868 cottage. It's a classic tea room, only they do lunches, not teas, serving one hot dish as well as soup, salads and sandwiches. Both the portions and the prices are reasonable, but the desserts are irresistibly rich. Recipes for two of them have appeared in *Bon Appetit* magazine. Lunching here fits perfectly into a day spent exploring historic Jacksonville.

*Wolf Creek Tavern*                                                             *866-2474*
*Off I-5 at Wolf Creek, 20 miles north of Grants Pass*
*Breakfast, lunch and dinner, Sunday brunch*
*Moderate prices*

Wolf Creek Tavern was built in about 1873 and acquired by the State Park Department a hundred years later, in very sad condition. It has been restored and is now operated as an inn. There are bedrooms with baths in a wing that was added in the 1920's, and one glorious room upstairs in the old part of the building which is furnished with 1870's pieces and is a bargain at $42.

Sunday brunch here was unusual but very good; instead of selecting from a menu with a choice of entrees, everyone was served the same meal, but there was a great variety of things included — eggs, ham, sausage, crepes with maple butter, juice, fresh fruit, muffins, even a small dessert. The dinner menu is more traditional and offers choices of roast beef, steak, seafood and pasta in the usual format.

Wolf Creek is about fifteen miles further north from Paradise Ranch, or about sixty five miles from Ashland. The historic exhibits in the inn are interesting in themselves, and it's close to I-5 if you're on your way somewhere else.

# *Where to Drink*

The local branch of the Women's Christian Temperance Union was organized by Ann Hill Russell, who, with her mother and sisters, came to Ashland in 1853. She seems to have been the town dynamo, but according to Marjorie O'Harra's town history, there were already five saloons in the 1880's in spite of the women's opposition. You won't have any problems finding a drink here today; bar's can stay open until 2:30 AM, and anyone over twenty-one can drink.

There are four bars in downtown Ashland. I'm sure there are differences in style that their habitues can recognize, but they all seem similarly dark and cozy. Snack food appears to be available in some of them. These four are:

*The Beau Club*
*347 East Main St., near Second St.*

*Cook's Tavern*
*66 East Main St., next to the festival Exhibit center*
Fish and Chips are advertised in the window.

*The Irish Pub*
*On East Main, next to Change of Heart*
A blackboard on the sidewalk announces the games to be seen on TV and offers New York Style Pizza.

*The Log Cabin Tavern*
*41 North Main St., on the plaza*

There is a popular cocktail lounge in the lobby of the Mark Antony:

*The Stage Door*
*212 East Main St.*

If any part of the hotel reopens, it should.

And several of the downtown restaurants also have bars:

*Alex's*
*35 North Main St., on the plaza*

A gorgeous long bar to belly-up to plus an attractive, airy seating area overlooking the plaza. A short list of mostly fried snacks is available.

*Beasy's Back Room*
*139 East Main St.*

A small but comfortable bar plus the whole dining area to sit in if you're going to eat; it closes with the restaurant.

*Chateaulin*
*50 East Main St., just south of the plaza*

A few stools at the back of the restaurant, under the stained glass maiden, plus the tables of course, when it's not crowded with diners. The selection of liqueurs and wines is large and the list of specialty coffees seems endless. Enough interesting snacks are served to construct a light meal, and good desserts are available, too.

*Jazmin's Bistro*
*180 C St.*

A nightclub, with a changing program of jazz, folk and rock music to go with your drinks.

*Jonathan's*
*132 North Main St., in the Bard's Inn*

Wine bar only, but in a lovely setting.

*Tommy's*
*47 North Main St., on the plaza*

A neat, square bar has been tucked into the center of the redesigned restaurant, with a few comfortable booths. It closes with the restaurant.

There are also bars and lounges in some of the outlying motels and restaurants:

*Callahan's Siskiyou Lodge*
*At the Mt. Ashland exit from I-5*

A big, friendly place with a deck for hot nights and a fireplace for when it's cold.

*Cascade Lounge*
*Ashland Hills Inn*
*2525 Ashland St., at the I5/Hwy 66 interchange*
Quite plush, like the motel it's in, with entertainment most nights and dancing on weekends.

*The Oak Knoll*
*3070 Highway 66, at the golf course, on the other side of I-5*
A friendly nineteenth hole.

*The Oak Tree Lounge*
*2365 Highway 66, near the I5 interchange*
Behind the Oak Tree Restaurant and similar in style.

*Omar's*
*1380 Siskiyou Blvd., near SOSC*
The bar is separate from the restaurant, stays open longer hours and retains more road-house feel.

## Supplies For Cooks and Picnickers

**BAKERIES**

*Ashland Bakery*
*340 A St., in the railroad district*
*38 East Main St., just off the plaza*
The production bakery and the cafe are both described under Light Meals. The bakery counters sell bread and a wide variety of croissants and sweet rolls. Assorted desserts are also available but the selection is unpredictable.

*The Bagel Man*
*1467 Siskiyou Blvd., in the Buy-Rite shopping center*
Mostly bagels, with cream cheese and drinks to go with them.

*The Breadboard Restaurant*
*744 North Main St.*
Cinnamon rolls and pies to go.

*Mana From Heaven Bakery*
*358 East Main St.*
San Franciscans familiar with The Court of the Two Sisters will understand why this is so good, being run by some of the same people.

*Munchies Restaurant*
*59 North Main St., on the plaza, below Gerry's Ice Cream*
A considerable selection of sweet baked goods, all remarkably huge and solid looking.

*Puck's Doughnuts*
*44 C St.*
*Opens and closes early, 6 AM to noon.*
All kinds of doughnuts.

*Safeway Bakery*
*(see below under Grocery Stores)*
Better than what you find in packages on the grocery shelves, but not up to real bakery standards.

*Thriftway Bakery*
*(see below under Grocery Stores)*
Much more variety and a bit higher quality than the Safeway bakery.

## CONVENIENCE STORES

*Ashland Country Grocery*
*917 East Main St.*
A small selection of oddly assorted items in an old building.

*Minute Markets*
*304 North Main St.*
*1690 Siskiyou Blvd.*
Open 7 AM to 12 Midnight
Newspapers, ice, microwaved snacks and miscellaneous groceries.

*7 - 11*
*1281 Siskiyou Blvd., near SOSC*
The fast food of groceries, the same all over

## GROCERY STORES

*Ashland Community Food Store*
*41 Third St., at Lithia Way*
*Open every day 9 AM to 8 PM*
A Co-op emphasizing natural and organically grown foods, health foods and vitamins, inexpensive sandwiches and picnic possibilities.

*Buy-Rite*
*1745 Siskiyou Blvd., just beyond the Hwy. 66 turnoff*

Lithia Park in winter; the paths are great for walking any time of year and the shaded lawns are are ideal for picnics in hot weather. *Ashland Chamber of Commerce, Medford Mail Tribune.*

*Open 7 days, 8 AM to 11 PM*
All the usual things including wine; ice machine outside.

*Namanny's Triple T Market*
*372 East Main St.*
An old-fashioned, downtown grocery store with a live butcher.

*Safeway*
*585 Siskiyou Blvd.*
*Open 24 house every day*
A gigantic store with a bakery and a delicatessen as well as all the usual packaged, fresh and frozen foods, housewares and wine.

*Sentry Market*
*Oak and A Sts.*
*Open 8 AM to 9 PM*

Not as neat and plastic as Safeway, but big, with a full range of groceries and a separate health food and vitamin department.

*Thriftway*
*1644 Ashland St., in the Ashland Shopping Center*
Another big store with a very complete bakery and an ice machine outside.

*U-Mark-It*
*2268 Hwy 66, in the shopping center between I-5 and the rail road*
*Open 7 days from 8 AM to 10 PM*
A warehouse style store with everything, including wine, but only a small meat department.

## Health Foods and Vitamins

*All's Well Herb and Vitamin Shop*
*77 Oak St., just below East Main St.*

*Ashland Community Food Store (see above under Grocery Stores)*

*Sunshine Corner*
*1650 Hwy 66, in the Ashland Shopping Center*
Health foods and vitamins.

*Sentry Market*
*(see above under Grocery Stores)*

## Juicery

*Pyramid Juice Co.*                                    482-2292
*160 Helman St., at Van Ness, two blocks north of Bard's Inn*
Open Tuesday to Saturday, 10 AM to 2 PM, June through September or by appointment. Taste and buy their unique fruit and vegetable juices and blends.

## Wine and Liquor Stores

*The Ashland Liquor Store*
*40 C St., at Oak St.*
The Oregon Liquor Control Commission Agency #12

*Ashland Wine Cellar*
*38 C St., downstairs below the liquor store*
*Open Monday to Saturday, 11 A.M. to 7 P.M.*
Tasting as well as sales.

*Valley View Tasting Room*
*52 East Main St., near the plaza*
*Open Tuesday through Saturday, 12 Noon to 5:30 PM*
Taste and buy the winery's products.

All the major grocery stores also carry wine and beer; Siskiyou Vineyards wines are also available at the Oregon Store, on the plaza.

## SPECIAL PICNICS

You can always do a brown bag picnic with grocery store food and utensils, or take something out from a delicatessen or fast food place, but for picnicking in style try:

Domingo Perozzi's Creamery circa 1897. *Southern Oregon Historical Society, Elhart Collection*

*Greenleaf Delicatessen*                                              *482-2808*
*49 North Main St.*

Box lunches and picnic baskets with several menus to choose from. The baskets contain a table cloth, glasses and utensils as well as the meal. Prices range from $5 to $12 per person, or you can design your own menu and pay the cost of the food plus a $5 rental charge for the equipment. A deposit of $20-25 is also collected to guarantee return of the basket.

*Ashland Hills Inn*                                                   *482-8310*
*2525 Ashland St., at I5 exit 14*         *ext. 179 for picnic baskets*
                                          *ext. 132 for a delivered lunch*

Three different picnic basket menus, each including your choice of wine, soda or sparkling cider, are offered at $10-15 per person. There is a $20-25 deposit on the basket which is equipped with wine glasses, napkins, silverware and a paring knife. Ashland Hills also has a lunch delivery service on weekdays. A variety of sandwiches and salads, from $3.95 to $5.95 and your choice of beverages, can be delivered to you; the minimum order is $10.

# Emergency Aid and Useful Services

---

EMERGENCIES

## Call 911 for fire, police or medical emergencies

Some other numbers to have and hope you never need:

- Ashland Community Hospital
  280 Maple St. — Go north on North Main;
  turn left on Maple

  | | |
  |---|---|
  | 24 hour emergency room: | 482-2441 |
  | TTY emergency number: | 488-1906 |

- Ambulance Service:       482-2882
- Poison Control Center (toll free):   1-800-452-7165
- Crisis Hotline: Rape, Suicide prevention:   779-4357
- Runaway Hotline (toll free):   1-800-231-6946

---

Below are the listings that should help you find the products and services that you may need while visiting Ashland, the boring essentials. There's not much fun in getting film developed or washing clothes, but having a list with addresses, directions and telephone numbers can help you save time for more interesting activities.

As downtown Ashland attracts more visitors and more businesses that cater to them — more amusing gift shops and fancy restaurants and sophisticated boutiques — the ordinary, resident oriented, businesses tend to locate where rents are lower. Some are scattered in the railroad district and along the major streets, North and East Main, Siskiyou and Ashland, and some are in the shopping centers.

There are three shopping plazas located along Highway 66 (Ashland St.), each one newer and bigger than the last as you go from Siskiyou Blvd. to the freeway. They tend to be the place for practical shopping rather than browsing for pleasure. There are grocery, superdrug and variety stores plus smaller useful services like film processing, copiers and video rentals. Starting from Siskiyou and heading out Ashland St. toward I-5, the shopping centers are:

First, Buy Rite Plaza, a single line of stores with a parking lot in front that runs between Siskiyou Blvd. and Ashland St., just past the point where Ashland St. turns off. Buy Rite grocery is at the Siskiyou end, and all the stores' addresses are on Siskiyou, but coming from downtown it's easier to turn left onto Ashland and then right into the parking lot.

Second, the somewhat bigger Ashland Center, where Thriftway market and Thrifty superdrug are located. The addresses here are on Ashland (Highway 66), but there is an entrance off Siskiyou, via a driveway next to Angelo's Pizza. If you're headed toward Ashland on Siskiyou, look for the Ashland Center sign on the right.

Third, the giant shopping center between the railway overpass and the freeway interchange, with the Bi-Mart superdrug and U-Mark-It grocery, and lots more. The address and the entrance are on Ashland St. but it doesn't seem to have a name. If you're near the southern end of Siskiyou Blvd., you can take Tolman Creek Road as the center is at the intersection of Tolman Creek Rd. and Ashland St.

If you really need something that you cannot find in Ashland, there is Medford, a much larger city with all sorts of resources, only fifteen miles away on I-5. Rogue Valley Mall, with three major department stores and about seventy other shops, is located near the North Medford exit from I-5. At times Ashland is so beguilingly peaceful that it's hard to believe that the modern world is that close, and even harder to go out and join it.

One word about opening and closing times: if you have to go out of your way and it's any time outside of weekday business hours, call first. Lots of places close early on Saturday afternoon; this really is a small town, still.

## ART SUPPLIES

*SOSC Bookstore*            *428-6178*

Upstairs in the Britt Building, above the information office, on Siskiyou Blvd.

## AUTOMOBILE DEALERS

Highway 99 north from Ashland seems to be auto row. In addition to the two dealerships listed, there are many specialized parts and repair firms in this area. Dealers in other makes of car can be found in Medford.

*Butler Ford/Peugeot*           *482-2521*
*1977 Highway 99 N*

Sales, rentals, leasing, parts, service and body work.

*Town & Country Chevrolet/Oldsmobile*      *482-2411*
*2045 Highway 99 N*

Sales, leasing, parts and service.

## BANKING

*Benjamin Franklin Savings and Loan*      *482-5411*
*101 East Main St., at the corner of Pioneer St.*

*First Interstate Bank*      *488-0431, 488-0435*
*67 East Main St., between Pioneer and Oak Sts.*

*Jackson County Federal Savings & Loan*      *482-2451*
*183 East Main St., near First St.*

*Klamath First Federal Savings & Loan*      *482-3045*
*512 Walker St., at Hwy 66*

*United States National Bank of Oregon*      *482-1522*
*30 North Second St., at East Main St.*

*Valley of the Rogue Bank*      *482-9611*
*250 Pioneer St., at B St.*

*Western Bank*
*243 East Main St.*      *482-4321*
*2262 Ashland St.*      *482-8336*

## BICYCLES

*Ashland Cycle Sport*      488-0581
*191 Oak St., at C St.*
Sales and service.

*Ashland Mountain Supply*      488-2479
*31 North Main St., on the plaza*
Sales, repairs and rentals (5 and 18 speed bikes available).

*Siskiyou Cyclery*      482-1997
*1729 Siskiyou Blvd., south of SOSC, near Harmony Lane*
Sales, repairs, and rentals (10 speeds).

## CAMERAS AND FILM PROCESSING

*Ashland Camera*      482-8743
*163 East Main St., across from the Varsity Theatre*

*Aurora Photographics*      488-0847
*116 C St., at Pioneer*

*Frodsham Photo Finishing*      488-2313
*Ashland Shopping Center, off Hwy 66*

*Rocket Photo*      488-0690
*C and Second Sts., one block from East Main*

*Total Camera*      482-1972
*1640 Ashland St., in the Ashland Shopping Center*

## CAR WASHES, DO IT YOURSELF STYLE

*Ashland Buggy Bath/Sofspra*      488-0093
*690 Harmony Lane*

*Sentry Car Wash*
*Sentry Market parking lot, Oak and A Sts.*

## CHURCHES AND RELIGIOUS ORGANIZATIONS

*Apostolic Lighthouse*      488-0496

*Ashland Bible Church*      482-8644
*400 Dead Indian Rd.*

To Medford and
Rogue Valley Mall

#19

RR

N. Main St.

I-5

N

3

2

E. Main St.

Hwy. 66

4 5

6

#14

Siskiyou Blvd.

#11

## Shopping Districts

1. North Main -- auto row plus miscellaneous small businesses
2. Downtown -- growing concentration of tourist oriented shops
3. Railroad District -- the Grange Co-op and scattered shops
4. Buy Rite Plaza -- very small shopping center
5. Ashland Center -- large selection of shops and services
6. Tolman Creek Rd./Ashland St. -- huge shopping center with fast food outlets

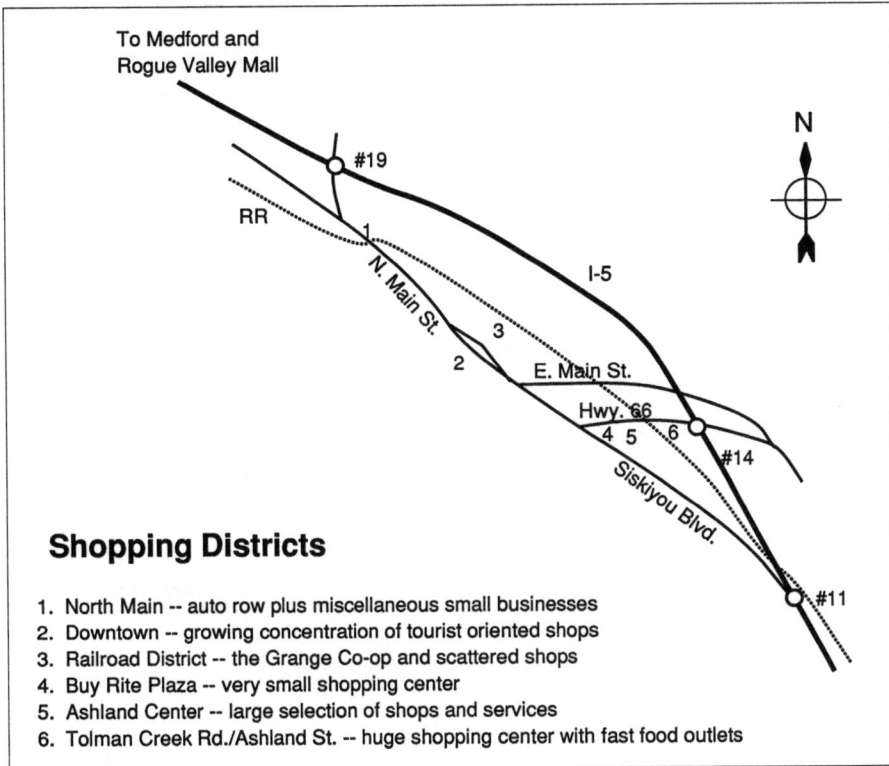

| | |
|---|---|
| *Ashland Christian Fellowship* | *482-8539* |
| *Nondenominational* | |
| *204 Hersey St.* | |
| *Ashland Missionary Baptist Church* | *482-1531* |
| *185 Mountain Ave.* | |
| *Bahai Faith* | *482-2488* |
| *351 E. Hersey St.* | |
| *Bellview Christian Church* | *482-8748* |
| *1033 Tolman Creek Rd.* | |
| *Calvary Baptist Church* | *482-4605* |
| *Southern Baptist* | |
| *2082 East Main St.* | |
| *Campus Christian Ministry* | *488-2304* |
| *1150 Ashland St.* | |

Christian Center Assembly of God          482-2456
188 Garfield St.

Christian Life Fellowship                 482-1227
Foursquare Church
599 East Main St.

Christian Missionary Alliance             482-1425
Bible Chapel
748 Siskiyou Blvd.

Christian Science Reading Room            482-2802
176 East Main St.

Church of Christ                          482-4635
621 Park St.

Church of Christ                          488-0483
84 Nevada St.

Church of Christ Christian                482-1561
318 B St.

Church of God                             482-5465
360 Cambridge St.

Church of Jesus Christ                    482-0100
of Latter Day Saints
111 Clay St.

Church of the Nazarene                    482-1784
87 Fourth St.

Circle of Friends Sufi Center      488-2715, 842-2073

Clay St. Community Church of God          482-4211
of Anderson, Indiana
631 Clay St.

Faith Tabernacle                          482-3411
840 Faith Ave.

Family Life Bible Church                  482-8052
Pentecostal Church of God
120 Sixth St.

Fire Baptized Holiness Church
583 Normal Ave.

| | |
|---|---|
| *First Baptist Church*<br>*American Baptist*<br>*2004 Siskiyou Blvd.* | *482-3836* |
| *First Church of Christ Scientist*<br>*1715 Ashland St.* | *488-0854* |
| *First Congregational*<br>*United Church of Christ*<br>*717 Siskiyou Blvd.* | *482-1981* |
| *First Presbyterian Church*<br>*Siskiyou Blvd. and Walker Ave.* | *482-3536* |
| *First United Methodist Church*<br>*North Main and Laurel Sts.* | *482-3647* |
| *Grace Lutheran Church*<br>*660 Frances Lane* | *482-1661* |
| *Kingdom Hall*<br>*Jehovah's Witnesses*<br>*700 North Main St.* | *482-5125* |
| *Newman Center*<br>*1150 Ashland St.* | *482-0852* |
| *Our Lady of the Mountain*<br>*Catholic Church*<br>*987 Hillview Dr.* | *482-1146* |
| *Rogue Valley Friends*<br>*1150 Ashland St.* | *482-4335* |
| *Rogue Valley Unitarian Universalist*<br>*Fellowship*<br>*2977 Barbara St.* | *482-4755* |
| *Seventh Day Adventist Church*<br>*1650 Clark St.* | *482-2226* |
| *Shir Hadash*<br>*Jewish Community Havura of Southern Oregon* | *482-8806* |
| *Temple Emek Shalom*<br>*1081 East Main St* | *488-2909* |

Trinity Episcopal Church 482-2656
44 North Second St.

Unity in Ashland 488-0890
563 North Main St.

Yeshe Nyingpo Vajrayana Buddhists 488-0477
1977 Colestin Rd.

## COMPUTERS AND ELECTRONICS

Radio Shack 482-2915
1638 Ashland St., Ashland Shopping Center, off Hwy. 66

## DENTISTRY — EMERGENCY SERVICE

Michael R Kempf 482-1741, 482-0290,
993 Siskiyou Blvd., Suite #3 482-1743 day or night

## HEARING AIDS

Ashland Audiology 482-1204
290 North Main St.

The Laundry and Cleaners circa 1915; the building has served as a hotel and a restaurant and currently houses Lithia Creek Arts and the New Playwrights Theatre. *Ashland Public Library, print by Terry Skib.*

*Siskiyou Audiology Center*  488-0628
*993 Siskiyou Blvd., Suite #2*

## LAUNDRY AND DRY CLEANING

*Archie's Fabric and Leather Care*  482-9202
*151 North Pioneer St., between B and C Sts.*
Dry cleaning.

*Campus Cleaners and Laundry*  482-2281
*1465 Siskiyou Blvd., in the Buy Rite plaza*
Economy dry cleaning by the pound and full service cleaning and pressing, shirt service, alterations, suede and leather care.

*Henry's Highlander Center Laundromat*
*1656 Ashland, in the Ashland Shopping Center*
Open 8 AM to 10 PM every day.

*The Laundry Room*  488-0703
*1465 Siskiyou Blvd., in the Buy Rite plaza*
Drop off and self service laundromat, open seven days, 7 AM to 9 PM.

*Pioneer Laundromat*  482-3349
*310 Pioneer, next to the Sentry Market*
Open 8 AM to 9 PM daily.

*Varney's Clothing Care Center*  482-4515
*1660 Siskiyou Blvd., near Walker St.*
Drop off and self service laundry, shirt service, dry cleaning, leather and suede cleaning, mending, tailoring and alterations. Open 7 AM to 10 PM seven days a week.

## MAPS

*Ashland Chamber of Commerce*  482-3486
*110 East Main St.*
A street map of Ashland with an index and readable type is $1.

*Northwest Nature Shop*  482-3421
*154 Oak St.*
A good selection of maps, including detailed ones suitable for hikers and waterproof ones for river touring.

*Rogue River National Forest*                              482-3333
*Ashland Ranger Station*
*645 Washington St.*

For $1 you can get a map of the Rogue River National Forest, showing both trails and roads; the rangers can also give you information about trail and road conditions.

## MUSIC AND INSTRUMENTS

*Cripple Creek Music Co.*                                  482-9141
*353 East Main St.*
Sales, rentals and repairs.

## OPTICIANS

*Ashland Eye Care*                                         482-3873
*450 Siskiyou Blvd.*

*Ashland Optometric Clinic*                                482-3466
*933 Siskiyou Blvd.*

*William S. Epstein, M.D.*                                 482-8100
*648 North Main St.*

## PET SUPPLIES

*Grange Co-op*                                             482-2143
*421 A St., at 4th, in the Railroad District*

## PHARMACIES AND SUPERDRUGS

*Anderson's Pharmacy*                                      482-2421
*253 East Main St.*

*Ashland (Rexall) Drug*                                    482-3366
*275 East Main St.*

*Bi-Mart Pharmacy*                                         482-8191
*2280 Hwy 66, in the shopping center nearest the I5 interchange*
An immense store with everything from TV sets to pet food.

*Ideal Drugs*                                              482-2886
*1471 Siskiyou Blvd., in the Buy Rite shopping center*

*Thrifty* 488-0633
*1670 Ashland St., in the Ashland Shopping Center*
The pharmacy is open only Monday through Friday, 10 AM to 6 PM

## PICNIC AND PARTY SUPPLIES

*Ashland Party & Wedding Supply* 482-4545
*1407 Hwy 99N*
Everything for an elegant picnic or a birthday away from home.
*Hallmark Card & Party Shop* 482-2181
*290 East Main St.*

## POST OFFICE

*U.S. Postal Service* 482-3986
*120 N. First St., at C St.*

## SERVICE STATIONS

| | |
|---|---|
| Arco | *I-5 / Hwy 66 interchange, exit # 14* |
| Bi-Mor | *1649 Ashland St. (Hwy 66)* |
| | *1515 Siskiyou Blvd., south of SOSC* |
| Chevron | *I-5 / Hwy 66 interchange, exit # 14* |
| | *461 South Valley View Rd., near Hwy 99N* |
| Exxon | *I-5 / Hwy 66 interchange, exit # 14* |
| | *1765 Siskiyou Blvd.* |
| | *75 C St., between Oak and Pioneer Sts.* |
| | *I-5 / Valley View Rd. interchange, exit #19* |
| Mobil | *Lithia Way and East Main* |
| | *595 North Main St., at Maple St.* |
| | *Highway 99 at the I5 exit #19 turnoff* |
| Shell | *I-5 / Hwy 66 interchange, exit # 14* |
| | *Siskiyou Blvd. at Walker St.* |
| | *I5 exit #19* |
| Texaco | *I-5 / Hwy 66 interchange, exit #14* |
| | *449 East Main St.* |
| Union 76 | *I-5 / Hwy 66 interchange, exit # 14* |
| | *1401 Siskiyou Blvd., at the Hwy 66 turnoff* |

## SHOE REPAIR

*Ashland Shoe Repair*                           482-1046
*264 East Main St.*

*Cobbler's Bench*                               482-4656
*27 South Second St., just above East Main St.*

## SPORTING GOODS, CLOTHES AND EQUIPMENT

*Ashland Fly Shop*                              488-1110
*689 Washington St., off Hwy. 66 near the Super 8 Motel*
Fishing supplies.

*Ashland Mountain Supply*                       488-2749
*31 North Main St., on the plaza*
Sports and outdoor clothing and equipment including tents and packs; skis also available to rent.

*Inside Edge*
*115 East Main St., near Pioneer St.*           482-8121
Athletic shoes and clothes, specially for tennis and skiing.

*1970 Ashland St. (Hwy 66)*                     482-0101
Ski rentals.

*Four Seasons Adventures*                       482-8352
*290 Helman St. at Hersey St.*
Equipment sales and rentals for a wide range of activities.

*Oak Knoll Public Golf Course Pro Shop*         482-4311
Equipment and apparel for golfers.

## STATIONERY AND OFFICE SUPPLIES

*The Mart*                                      482-1181
*264 E. Main St.*

## SUN GLASSES

*Sunglass Connection*                           488-2758
*40 North Main St., in the Orchard Lane Mall*

# TIRES

Glen's Tire Center                                      482-4042
1383 Highway 99 N

Ross Johnson Tire Center                               482-2381
1896 Highway 66, at Park St.
Retreading and repair, too.

Les Schwab Tire Center                                482-4181
2308 Ashland St. (Hwy 66), between I5 and the railroad overpass
Retreading and repair, also batteries, shocks and brake service.

# TOURIST INFORMATION AND TRAVEL

Ashland Directory                                     482-5670
You may find it in your motel room or at your bed and breakfast inn.
Large type and clear layouts, plus the fact that only Ashland people and
businesses are included, make it much easier to use than the telephone
book. It includes a good map and entertaining trivia about the town, but
is not totally accurate.

Ashland Chamber of Commerce                        482-3486
110 East Main St., next to the Black Swan Theatre
Also at the plaza kiosk during the summer season
Informative leaflets on local facilities and literature from many local
businesses and attractions available free; they also sell a folding town map
with street index and street numbering for $1.

Explorer Travel Service                               488-0333
541 East Main St.

Lithia Travel                                         482-9341
850 Siskiyou Blvd.

The Town Crier
On East Main St., at Oak St., across from the ramp to the festival
Also in the Ashland Hills Inn lobby
These are computer terminals; the one downtown is accessible from
the sidewalk. It's an easy system to use, with menus and simple letter
commands. Since businesses pay to be listed, it's not totally complete,
but there is lots of information. There are also quite valuable discount
coupons which the computer will print out for ten cents each.

## Towing — 24 hour services

| | |
|---|---|
| *Bob's Towing* | *482-5845* |
| *Bounds 66 Exxon Service* | *482-3166, 482-5947* |
| *Star 24 Hour Towing* | *482-7827* |

## Veterinary Clinics

*Animal Medical Hospital*  *482-2786*
*1525 Highway 99 N*
*Veterinarian Leo J. van Dijk*

*Ashland Veterinary Hospital*  *482-1386*
*1645 Highway 66*
*Veterinarians Richard Hill and Dennis E. Sweet*

*Bear Creek Animal Clinic*  *488-0120*
*1955 Ashland St. (Hwy 66)*
*Veterinarian Howard Miller*

*Creekside Veterinary Hospital*  *482-2844*
*112 Helman St.*
*Veterinarian James R. Langhofer*

# *Update — May 1988*

The rate of changes in Ashland seems to have accelerated in the last six months:

**Closed:**
Archie's Pizza (the best pizza in town), Comic Relief (comic books), Gamekeepers (restaurant), La Burrita (Mexican restaurant — no loss), Mr. Popcorn (snack shop — no surprise), Mustard's Last Stand (hot dogs), Namanny's Triple T Market (groceries), the New Playwrights Theatre (the founding director left for bigger things), Ragamuffin (children's clothes), Sun Glass Connection (sun glasses), Titania's Carousel (gifts), Tug's Fish and Chips (the only fish and chips store in town), the Waterhole Lounge (the bar at the Cedarwood Motel).

**Moved:**
All's Well Herbs and Vitamins, down the block to 107 Oak St.; The Beanery (coffee and snacks), next door, to a larger space at 1602 Ashland St.; China Station, to 75 N. Main St., where Archie's Pizza used to be; Desert Republic (clothes), across the street to 161 E. Main, where Ragamuffin was; Plymale Cottage (Jacksonville restaurant), to the McCully House, at 240 E. California St., Jacksonville, where it's called the McCully House Cafe (new number: 899-1942).

**Changed Hands:**
Cascade Wildlife Gallery is now Rusty Drake Gallery and sells jewelry and Indian artifacts as well as prints; Cesar's Mexican Restaurant is reopening as Theresa's Cantina and Grill; Gerry's Homemade Ice Cream has become Ashland Fudge and Ice Cream, selling both ice cream and candy made on the premises.

## Opened:

Archibald's Tasting Room, 297 E. Main St. (where Mr. Popcorn was), Rogue Valley wines and gourmet foods; The Crepe Palace, various filled crepes, sold from the hole in the wall on the plaza where Mustard's Last Stand was; Designs in Leather, 80 N. Main St., custom leather clothing; Gallery Obscura, Visionary Art and Crystals, 505 Siskiyou Blvd,; Key of C, 116 C St., espresso and bagels; Leather and Lacey, 31 Water St., (in part of the Lithia Creek Arts space), gifts and handbags; Odus Magoo's, 14 S. First St. (where Titania's Carousel was), athletic shoes and sportswear; Rebel's Quichery, 5 Granite St. (formerly Tug's Fish and Chips), serving various quiches with salad and beverages; Sandy's $10 store, 264 Main St., sportswear for $10 or less; Studio X (a new theatre) at the Performing Arts Center, 208 Oak St., 488-2011; Tights and Tards, 77 Oak St., exercise and dance clothes.

## Opening Soon:

Ashland Ales, 31 Water St. (in the New Playwrights old space), a brewery pub; Fox House B&B, 269 B St., Wimer Street Inn, 75 Wimer St., 488-2319, a B&B with four rooms and private baths.

What next?

# *Acknowledgements*

I thought I knew a lot about Ashland when I started to plan this guide. What I quickly learned is how much I didn't know and how many opportunities for enhancing our family's time here had passed us by, unrecognized. I could not have gathered all this information without a lot of help. People at the Oregon Shakespearean and Britt Music Festivals, at Southern Oregon State College and the Southern Oregon Historical Society, and members of the community were so very generous with their time and their knowledge.

In particular I want to thank: William Patton, Executive Director, Paul Barnes, then Education Director, Carol Jones, Box Office Manager, and Kim Kalapus, Public Relations Assistant, of the Oregon Shakespearean Festival; Alan Armstrong, Director of the Shakespearean Studies Program, Dale Luciano, Chairman of the Theatre Arts Department, Meredith Reynolds, Coordinator of the Elderhostel Program, of Southern Oregon State College; Nan Hannon and Jean Vondracek at the Chappell-Swedenburg Museum and Carol Harbison and Karalee Newberg at the Jacksonville Museum of the Southern Oregon Historical Society; Kerry Hoover, Public Relations Director of the Peter Britt Festivals; william Elhart, whose photographs are housed at the Chappell-Swedenburg Museum, and Terry Skibby, curator of the Ashland Library's photo collection; Marjorie O'Harra, local historian and author; Anne Thomas, theatre critic for the Ashland Daily Tidings, and the people involved in various music and theatre groups with whom I talked; Sonja Akerman of the Ashland Department of Community Development, and the staff of the Ashland Park Department; and the reference librarians at the Ashland Public Library and Southern Oregon State College. All of them, along with the Festival volunteers, merchants, restaurateurs and innkeepers who answered my questions and volunteered information I didn't even know enough to ask for, have made this book possible.

Several publications have been very useful in preparing this guide, both as sources of information and for suggestions of places to investigate further: The *Ashland Daily Tidings* and its Supplements; Bridget Beattie McCarthy's Where to Find the *Oregon in Oregon; The Ashland Directory;* "Living and Doing Business in Ashland," published by the Chamber of Commerce; *Northwest Best Places* by David Brewster; Southern Oregon Salesman's "1987 Tourist Tips;" *The Great Towns of the Pacific Northwest* by David Vokac; *The Sunset Travel Guide to Oregon;* Marjorie O'Harra's *Ashland: The first 130 Years* and *Southern Oregon: Short Trips Into History;* Kay Atwood and L. Scott Clay's "Tour of Ashland, Oregon and Environs" for the Northern Pacific Coast Chapter of the Society of Architectural Historians; *The Ashland Area and its Environs,* an unpublished University of Oregon thesis by G Byron Backas. I have also relied on various Shakespeare Festival publications and their extensive press packet, and on the Peter Britt Festivals Silver Jubilee Program, for information.

I also want to thank my friends who contributed their expertise to this project: Philip Wood of Ten Speed Press/Celestial Arts, for his encouragement at the outset; Gerald Walker of York University, Toronto, for advice on drawing maps by computer; Susan Stern Cerny of the Berkeley Architectural Heritage Association, for information on historic preservation and walking tours and Lynda Schmidt for help with questions about RV's.

Susan Cerny, Lynda Schmidt, Pamela Ford, my daughters Susan Lundin and Rebecca Kun, and my husband, Robert Lundin, all read drafts and provided valuable, though sometimes brutal, editing, for which I am truly grateful. And most of all, I want to acknowledge my debt to my husband who put up with this project with great patience. If he hadn't shared my zany taste in honeymoons, we might never have discovered Ashland.

Of course, none of the people who helped me are responsible for any of the errors that you may find here. By the time you read this some restaurant will have closed, some new bed and breakfast inn will have opened — Ashland is not going to hold still in order to keep this guide current. And I will have goofed, probably more than once. So you are invited, urged, begged, to send me a postcard, at Box 7123, Berkeley, CA 94707, with the correct information. Even if its just a matter of disagreeing with my assessment of some motel or restaurant, I'd like hear your side of it. So please write; maybe you'll earn an acknowledgement in the next edition.

# *Index*

# NOTES

# NOTES

# NOTES

# NOTES

# NOTES

# NOTES